BeesKnees #4:
A Beekeeping Memoir

Volume Four: Days 301 - 400

The Journey of a Beginning Beekeeper

Fran Stewart

BeesKnees #4: A Beekeeping Memoir
Fran Stewart
© 2019

All rights reserved. No part of this book may be used or reproduced in any manner whatsoever without written permission from the author, except by a reviewer who may quote brief passages in a review.

Cover design by Darlene Carter

ISBN: 978-1-951368-04-3

This book was printed in the United States of America.

Published by
My Own Ship Press
PO Box 490153
Lawrenceville GA 30049

myownship@icloud.com
franstewart.com

*To the memory of my dad,
who taught me to swing a hammer*

Books by Fran Stewart

The Biscuit McKee Mystery Series:

Orange as Marmalade
Yellow as Legal Pads
Green as a Garden Hose
Blue as Blue Jeans
Indigo as an Iris
Violet as an Amethyst
Gray as Ashes
Red as a Rooster
Black as Soot
Pink as a Peony
White as Ice

A Slaying Song Tonight

The Scot Shop Mysteries:

A Wee Murder in My Shop
A Wee Dose of Death
A Wee Homicide in the Hotel

Poetry:

Resolution

For Children:

As Orange As Marmalade/
Tan naranja como Mermelada
(a bilingual book)

Non-Fiction:

From The Tip of My Pen: a workbook for writers
BeesKnees #1: A Beekeeping Memoir
BeesKnees #2: A Beekeeping Memoir
BeesKnees #3: A Beekeeping Memoir
BeesKnees #4: A Beekeeping Memoir

Introduction to BeesKnees #4

When I began this jaunt into the world of beekeeping, I thought I knew what I'd be up against. At least I sort of thought I knew. What's that old saying about God laughing when people make plans?

I've always believed, though, that roadblocks lead to scenic detours and that good can come out of every situation, regardless of what our first reactions might be.

<<Sigh>>

You'll see what I'm talking about as we head further along this bee path. I'm so glad you're accompanying me on the journey.

I sincerely hope you're enjoying it as much as I am!

    --Fran
    from my house beside a creek
    on the other side of Hog Mountain GA

 Day #301 Answers to the Day 298 Questions
Tuesday, August 9, 2011

Time for the answers to our lighthearted moment from a few days ago:

|R|E|A|D|I|N|G| = reading between the lines

WEAR
LONG   = long underwear

B   E   E   = b flat

and finally,
O
M.D.
B.S.
Ph.D.   = 3 degrees below zero

Congratulations to Sherry, David, and Marie, who got all of them right!

We'll be back to talking about bees tomorrow . . .

BeeAttitude for Day #301: *Blessed are those who share their homes with rescued animals, for they shall receive unconditional love in return.*

Day #302 Africanized Bees
Wednesday, August 10, 2011

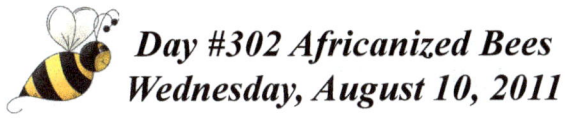

We had a bee club meeting Tuesday evening, and the speaker was talking about Africanized honeybees. They used to be called Killer Bees. Beekeepers frequently refer to them as Assassin Bees.

Very interesting. He gave us a lot of pointers about how to lessen the chances of our hives getting invaded by Africanized bees.
 Don't collect wild swarms (since they are more likely to be Africanized)
 Be sure your queens are marked, so you'll know whether or not a wild queen gets into your hive. If she does, you'll have to – gulp – squash her.
 Prevent swarms from your own hives

What to do if you run into Africanized bees and they start to run after you:
 Keep a garden sprayer of soapy water handy
 Run like crazy. The farther you run, the less likely they are to follow you.
 Get inside something – a house, a car – and close the door as fast as you can
 Use the sprayer! Soapy water kills bees. Don't worry if the inside of your car gets wet.
 Teach your children/spouse/friends these same rules

Then, he gave us a lot of pointers about how to BEE Friendly with our neighbors.
 Keep hives away from property lines
 Give the neighbors HONEY !
 Build a tall barrier around the hives so the bees have to fly up and over (that way they won't zoom across the neighbor's backyard grill)
 Give the neighbors HONEY ! !
 Give your bees a nearby water source *(like my leaky rain barrel)* so they won't fly into the neighbor's swimming pool – *that is NOT a problem in my poolless neighborhood!*
 Give the neighbors HONEY ! ! ! ! !

Fence your yard
Give the neighbors ... HONEY ! ! ! ! ! ! !

BeeAttitude for Day #302: *Blessed are those who those who treat wild bees with respect, for they shall live (relatively) stingfree.*

Day #303 Bee Flight and Space Flight
Thursday, August 11, 2011

One of the nicest things about bees—and there are MANY great things about bees to choose from—is the way they fly, particularly on their orienting flights, when they leave the hive for the first time. They circle around and around, making sure they know precisely where home is so that later on in life, when they're three weeks old and begin to forage far from the hive, they'll know what to come back to and where it is.

Wednesday morning I went outside at 5:45 to be sure I was in place for the 5:48 to 5:50 flyover time of the International Space Station. I found that exact time on NASA's ISS Tracker site. Go to "Sighting Opportunities," enter your country, and continue from there. *[2019 Note: I couldn't find this site anymore. Good luck finding it yourself.]*

As I watched the space station fly over, I couldn't help but think that all our space flights so far (and I vividly recall the very first one) must look, to beings far from Earth, like the orienting flights of bees *[See Day #208 5/8/2011]*.

There is the bright, shining space station, circling around and around its Earth hive, accompanied by millions of bit of debris that previous flights have left up there—dust, bits of paint flakes, and lots of bigger pieces, too. These bigger pieces (anything more than 10 centimeters in diameter) are what contribute to the "Kessler Syndrome." This syndrome states the possibility that eventually we'll fill the space around us with so much dangerous junk, that future space flights will be at risk or downright impossible because of the imminent possibility of collisions.

Here are two pictures of space waste that I lifted from the NASA site and good ole Wikipedia.

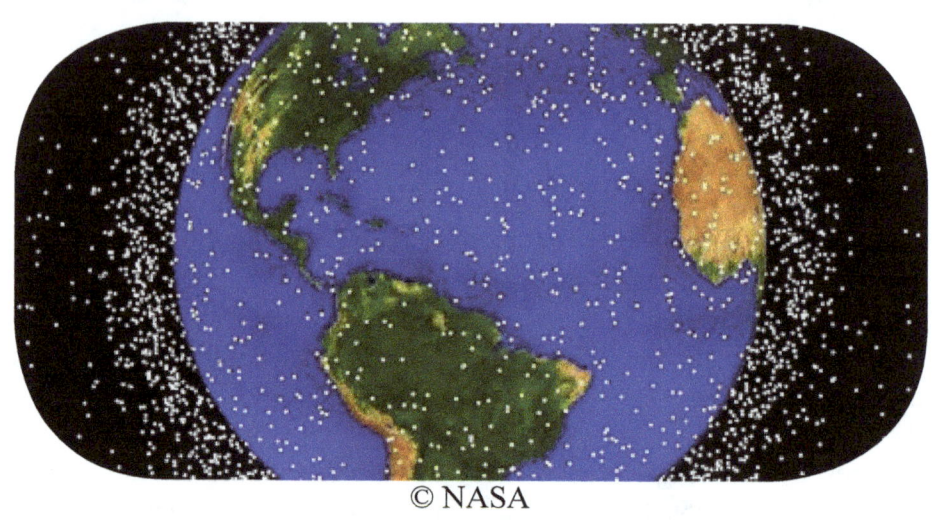
© NASA

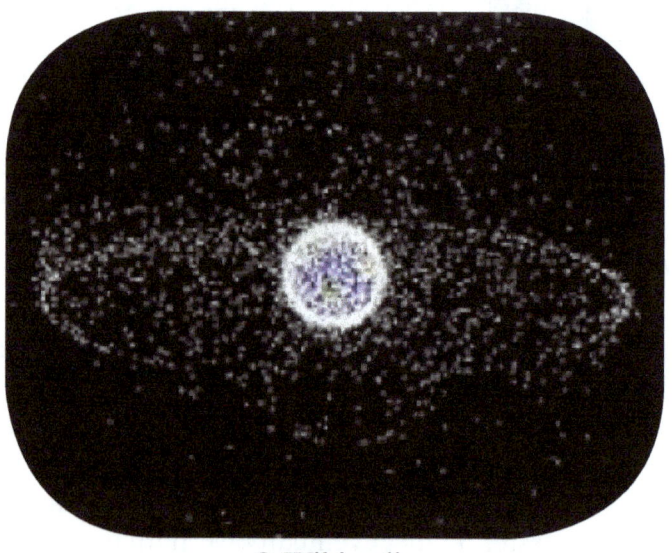
© Wikipedia

Neither one is a very pretty picture, eh?

So, in that way, we are *not* like bees. Just about the only space debris bees leave is bee poop [See Day #86]. They don't poop in their own hives—there's a *big* difference between bees and people! And bee poop is biodegradable, unlike the metal and plastic waste we tend to leave behind us, both above earth and on it.

Still, the ISS was gorgeous in that predawn hour, and seeing it was well worth the early trip to the end of my driveway.

Now, over the upcoming weekend, I hope to see the Perseides Meteor Shower. If I do, I'll let you know for sure.

BeeAttitude for Day #303: *Blessed are those who clean up after themselves, for they shall walk and not stumble.*

Fran Stewart

Day #304 Kisses from Two Very Different Critters
Friday, August 12, 2011

Awright, I know this may sound weird, but this morning, when Miss Polly woke me up by gently touching her paw to my cheek, I couldn't help but think about a fly that got in the house a couple of days ago and ended up landing on my cheek – not for very long, of course, since I batted it away.

But the fact that two such very different creatures both touched my cheek led me to wonder what a fly looked like close up. I had already taken a picture of Polly's nose as she sat beside me on the couch, and I located (on the MicroAngela website, the same place I found the microscopic photo of a honeybee head for Day #294) this picture that was labeled "Fly Kiss." *[2019 Note: The MicroAngela site is no longer active]*

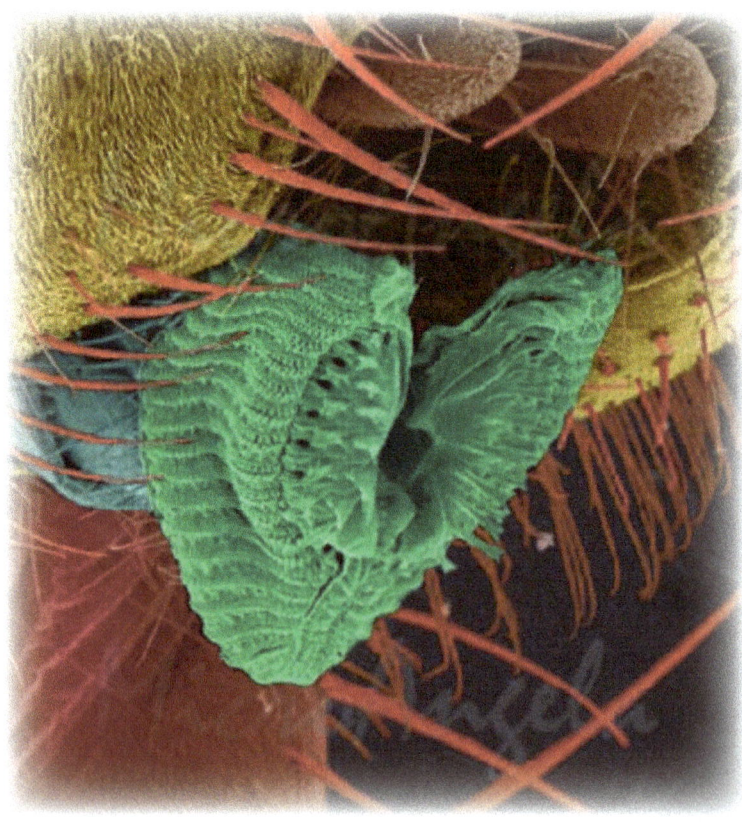

Copyright by Tina (Weatherby) Carvalho— MicroAngela

Polly Nose

Thought you might like to compare the two.

Given a choice, I'll take Miss Polly's nose any day.

I wonder what a fly looks like to a honeybee?

BeeAttitude for Day #304: *Blessed are those who think of fun analogies, for they shall entertain themselves.*

Fran Stewart

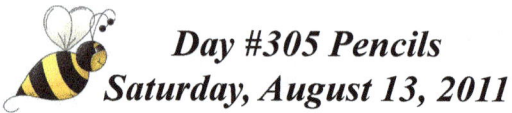

Day #305 Pencils
Saturday, August 13, 2011

Yesterday morning I stepped outside early, early, early. It was light enough to see but not light enough to start getting too hot. So I sat down at the table on my deck to listen to the bees for a while. It was so nice out there that I walked back inside to get the manuscript I'm working on. Give me some paper and a pencil and I'm pretty happy.

That got me to thinking about the common pencil. It's a truly marvelous invention, and it's been around since 1565. Anything that's lasted that long must have a few things going for it. Here are just a few I thought of. Let me know if you can think of any others.

A pencil is portable.
It runs without batteries. For that matter, it can run without brains, but I hope that's not the case here.
It has an eraser, the 1565 version of a delete key, although the attached eraser wasn't patented until 1858. Before that people used a separate eraser.
A pencil provides a handy canvas for tooth imprints. I've never known anyone who hasn't occasionally chewed on a pencil. What computer keyboard gives you that kind of alleviation? I don't group solitaire, Pac-Man, or minesweeper in the same league with a yellow number 2 Ticonderoga.
It can be thrown across the path / room / deck when simple deletion or chewing is not active enough (see the previous two notes above).
It can be sharpened without a fancy gadget. My Swiss Army knife works just fine. In a pinch I can even sacrifice a fingernail to tear the wood back away from the graphite.
It can be broken in half to fit in a tiny notebook or a small pocket. Of course, this eliminates the delete function of onehalf of it.
And, since it doesn't beep or ring, it will never scare my bees.

What a handy little tool!

BeeAttitude for Day #305: *Blessed are those who use pencils, for we bees appreciate their silence.*

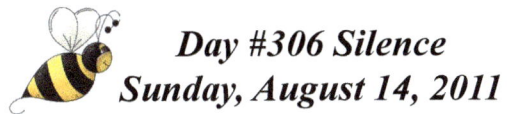
Day #306 Silence
Sunday, August 14, 2011

I think it would be safe to say that most people associate silence with nighttime. Fiftyfour years ago, in October of 1957, when I was in fifth grade, my father bundled me up in a gray and black blanket late one night and took me outside to watch the sky over Colorado Springs. Sputnik, the first humanmade orbiting intrusion into space, tumbled its way across the background of stars. (In 1957 one could still see jillions of stars.) Against their spangles, Sputnik skipped in eerie silence. Eerie because I was old enough to have picked up on my parents' fears about the possible launch of ballistic missiles.

In school over the next number of months, we had drills in which we sat—in silence, another kind of silence—beneath our desks with our heads ducked beneath our arms for protection. That was a silence stippled with fear and later, when the drills became old hat, and when we realized the enormity of what a nuclear attack would entail, with desks as scant protection, those were silences laced with derision.

We all have had numerous instances of silence in our lives. The silence of sitting next to a sick child, listening to each labored breath. The silence of that moment when we know the fever has turned and all will be well. The silence of sitting with a dying parent, knowing that the next breath might be the last. The silence of hearing that last breath and waiting for another that will never come. The silence of walking through a woodland park, unaware of the thunder from the interstate just one mile away, listening to the multifaceted silence of bird song, coupled with the awareness that that particular kind of silence used to be a lot louder before pesticides and fertilizers and clear cutting destroyed so many of our songbirds.

There is the silence now when we may sit with quiet around us, yet feel bombarded by questions and concerns from within, from which we cannot rid ourselves.

I find I much prefer the buzzy silence of my bees as I listen and almost don't listen because I'm getting so used to their sound.

There is the silence now of ending this blog post—my writing it, your reading it.

What silences do you remember and which ones have you forgotten to remember?

BeeAttitude for Day #306: *Blessed are those who know how to be quiet in their own minds, for they shall radiate peacefulness to others.*

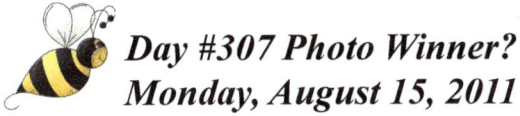 Day #307 Photo Winner?
Monday, August 15, 2011

Well, it seems the very favorite photo I've posted so far on this blog is the one of me kissing Lacy the Chicken. From the numbers of emails and phone calls I've gotten about it, I think it's a clear winner. But if you'd like to vote for a different photo, like the one of me being downed by the police dog, the milkweed pod, Sparrow in the sink, the slurpy cow, or the thistle seeds in my granddaughter's hair, or any of the others that I've used in these posts, be sure to let me know.

What's been your favorite photo so far?

BeeAttitude for Day #307: *Blessed are those who praise where praise is due, for they shall promote praiseworthy behavior.*

Fran Stewart

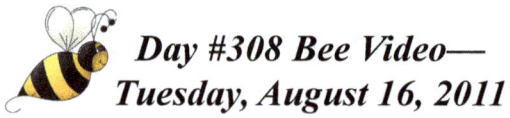

Day #308 Bee Video—
Tuesday, August 16, 2011

My friend Darlene Carter sent me a link to a fascinating bee video, and I wanted to share it with you. I watched the whole thing (all 42 minutes of it, including the commercials).

If you manage to get through to the end, it will be well worth it. There are loads of incredibly detailed videos of honeybees inside the hive. At the very end you'll see a brand new baby bee emerging from her cell and being cleaned up by nurse bees. I almost cried seeing it.

https://www.snagfilms.com/films/title/the_nature_of_things_bee_talker_the_secret_world_of_bees

There's one segment in here about bees as artists/sculptors.

You'll see Dr. Mark Winston and some of his science students in the field experimenting with pheromones by removing a queen bee and observing how long it takes her workers to find her. (Hint: not long!)

Did you know Aristotle was a biologist? News to me!

BeeAttitude for Day #308: *Blessed are those who are kind to hairy winged creatures, for we shall pollinate their world.*

BeeAttitude footnote: *Bees are hairy. Wasps are not.*

BeesKnees #4: A Beekeeping Memoir

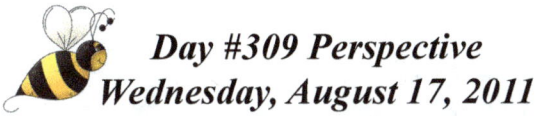 ***Day #309 Perspective***
Wednesday, August 17, 2011

Don't let perspective fool you. You never know what might be around the corner – or under the overhang.

When I look down on my hives, I see this:

Looks like there aren't many bees, right?

Ah, but I need to shift my perspective a bit, see the other side of this story.

When I look sideways at the hive, I see this:

sorry the picture's fuzzy...

Funny what a little shift like that will reveal.

What can you look at from a different angle today?

BeeAttitude for Day #309: *Blessed are those who look at life from many perspectives, for they shall remain flexible all their lives.*

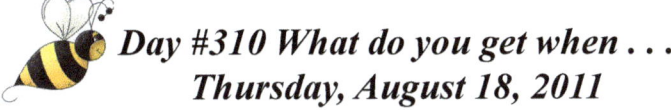
Day #310 What do you get when...
Thursday, August 18, 2011

a. I had a faucet replaced recently by my favorite plumber people, Keep Smiling Plumbing.

b. I caught two bees inside my house Wednesday night. They were looking for a way back out, of course, so I clapped a little plastic container over them (one at a time) and ushered them back outside.

c. These two events got me to thinking ...

What do you get when you cross a bee with a plumber?

BeeAttitude for Day #310: *Blessed are those who return lost bees, for they shall sleep better.*

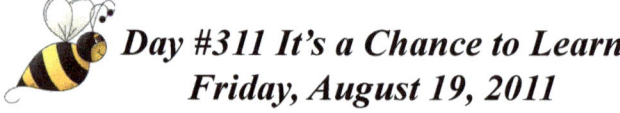

Day #311 It's a Chance to Learn
Friday, August 19, 2011

That's what I keep telling myself. This is a chance to learn.

Thursday afternoon I opened the brown/white hive. That's the one that started out as a very inadequate nuke, worth less than half what I paid for it – but that's another story. I've been reluctant to open the hives, afraid of what I'd find, but I finally screwed up my courage and . . .

What I found was:

1. When I opened the box, the bees didn't do that excited buzzy buzzy thing they usually do when they're disturbed. It was as if they had no energy whatsoever.

2. Top box (the supposed honey "super" where the bees were supposed to store extra honey) – there was still nothing in the super. Nothing at all. They hadn't drawn out a bit of comb. The five frames were as empty as the day I put them in there.

3. Middle box – this was the upper of two brood chambers, those two bottom boxes where the bees are supposed to do all their baby rearing. There were lots of bees, but they were as lethargic as could be. They didn't object at all when I pulled out the frames one at a time. One frame was completely empty. The other four had some capped brood, the cells with brownish-colored caps where baby bees are getting ready to hatch.

4. The bad news was that there were no eggs, no larvae, no honey, and no pollen, which means that when those baby bees do hatch, they'll starve to death. And as the older bees die off, there will be no younger ones to replace them unless the queen starts laying eggs pretty soon.

5. Oh yes, the queen. I didn't see her. If there's no queen, the hive will die out.

6. There's hope, because I didn't open the bottom brood chamber. I was

too discouraged by the top one. There's a possibility the queen is down there, waiting out this dry spell, knowing that there's not enough forage to feed an increased population.

So – what did I do? I plopped a big quart jar of sugar water on there. At least that will keep them from starving, and give the emerging babies something to eat. As to whether or not the queen will make it – we'll just have to wait and see.

I'm going to open the box again next Tuesday. Please send good wishes—and prayers if you're the praying sort. My bees can use all the help they can get.

BeeAttitude for Day #311: *Blessed are those who learn as they go, for they shall find lessons all around them.*

 ## *Day #312 Drinking Like Crazy*
Saturday, August 20, 2011

The good news is that the bees are alive enough to be drinking like crazy.

I went from an absolutely full quart jar of sugar water to this in less than 18 hours:

Of course they're still not hanging out much:

But if they're consuming that much sugar water, there's hope.

BeeAttitude for Day #312: *Blessed are those who enjoy our favorite writer (Shakespeare), who said "To bee or not to bee, that is the question."*

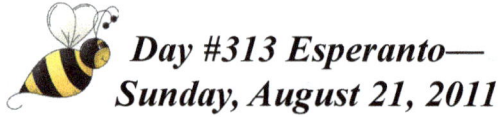
Day #313 Esperanto—
Sunday, August 21, 2011

When I was having a cup of tea at Aris*tea*crats a few weeks ago, I spotted a book on Esperanto, the universal language. I'd heard about Esperanto, but hadn't ever looked into it. I have to admit, I'm fascinated by the idea. And I'm pretty sure that if I had a friend who showed any interest in it, I'd probably devote some time to learning it.

It's so doggone logical. Each vowel has ONE sound, for instance. Each consonant has ONE sound.

That reminded me of a little word game my children played on me when they were in high school. Here it is:

What's this word? GHOTI

I'm willing to bet you're saying something like

goatee

gotee

guhhoetee, or even

joetee.

Uh huh. It's FISH.

"How's that?" you ask.

Well, you take the sound of

"gh" as in lau**gh**,

"o" as in w**o**men, and

"ti" as in nation

Put all three of those sounds together, and you get FISH.

Esperanto is much easier to figure out than that. For one thing, every noun ends in –o. For plural, you add a –j.

one book=unu libro

two books=du libroj

three books=tri libroj

four cats=kvar katoj

kvin sinjoroj—gentlemen

ses virinoj—women

sep ĵurnaloj—newspapers

ok avantaĝoj—advantages

naŭ ideoj—ideas

dek bovinoj—cows

and – I have to add this one: 30 mil abeloj = 30 thousand bees

So, what does this have to do with beekeeping?

Years ago I read about a woman traveling in Germany. Walking down a residential street one day, she stopped to admire a beautiful garden. The woman working in the garden looked up, smiled. They quickly discovered that they had no knowledge of each other's language until one of them pointed to a flower and called it by its botanical name. From there they happily wandered through her profuse garden, sharing the names in Latin, a very old common tongue.

I wonder what beekeepers do at international meetings? I doubt anybody there speaks Latin. Surely Esperanto would help.

Wonder if I can find a class somewhere?

BeeAttitude for Day #313: *Blessed are those who learn another language, for they shall have their horizons widened.*

Day #314 Looking to Plant — What???
Monday, August 22, 2011

I've been thinking a lot about my front yard, wondering how I can make it more bee friendly. The reason I'm thinking this is that a catalog from *Wayside Gardens* appeared in my mailbox Saturday.

The trouble is – my front yard is so small, I have to be careful what I plant. Anything too big will simply overwhelm it. That's a lesson I learned the hard way. This fall I'm going to be taking out two confederate roses (they get ten feet tall and very bushy, and bloom in the late, late summer for a very short time). I doubt they have much bee value, but I'll wait until after they bloom. If the bees like them I may reconsider.

And then there are those daylilies. All summer long—and I must admit they do have a fairly long blooming season—I never saw a single honeybee on them. Out of there! If anybody wants them, let me know. All you have to do is come over and help me dig them up.

I have a whole row of Rose of Sharon trees that were here when I bought the house. Do you have any idea how many seedlings those things give off? Good grief, I could pull up fifty and would still be behind. The bees visit them occasionally, but never look like they're very enthusiastic about it.

What to replace them with, though? I'm going to Google "beefriendly plants Georgia" and see what I get.

Wish me luck.

BeeAttitude for Day #314: *Blessed are those who feed the hungry (bees) when we are in danger of starving, for we shall (someday) make honey for them.*

bee.s. Thank you for the sugar water. It doesn't have any pollen, but we'll take what we can get this time of year.

Day #315 The First Major Pollinators
Tuesday, August 23, 2011

Now, since this is a blog about bees and beekeeping, I'll bet you think I'm going to say the first major pollinators were honeybees—or bumble bees—or mason bees.

Nope!

Several hundred million years ago, before there were bees to pollinate the plants, guess what critter filled that ecological niche?

Are you ready for this?

Mosquitoes!

I would imagine that means mosquitoes were there to feed the first birds and frogs, too, when those came along.

So, the next time you're outside slapping away at those pesky little skeeters who are after your blood, how 'bout you thank them before you squash them?

BeeAttitude for Day #315: *Blessed are those who slow down at night in case there are deer crossing the road, for they shall be safer as a result.*

 ## Day #316 One More Sting
Wednesday, August 24, 2011

Kaphooey! I went outside Tuesday morning to collect the empty hummingbird feeder. Lots of bees were buzzing around it. I lifted it from its hook, made sure no bees were still on it, and walked inside. As I turned I must have brushed my hand against a bee who'd taken a liking to my slacks.

I now have a red swollen area on my leg as big as my hand—my WHOLE hand.

Fortunately, I didn't have an allover reaction. I do have that epi pen on hand just in case, but I'd really rather not need it.

Tomorrow morning as I'm coming inside, I'd better check my clothes in a mirror before I move! I don't want any more bees to die as a result of my carelessness.

BeeAttitude for Day #316: *Blessed are those who watch where they put their hands, for they shall be safer in the long run.*

Day #317 Successful Hive Inspection!
Thursday, August 25, 2011

It's amazing what a little sugar water will do for a starving colony. I'm not talking about how people run in the door and yell, "What's for dinner? I'm starving!"

I'm talking about 60,000 bees too exhausted and depleted even to buzz when I opened their lid. That was last week, though. After seven days of sugar water feeding (I went through an entire 10pound bag of sugar), the queen has started laying again, and the bees are happy and buzzy once more.

Thanks to my beekeeping mentor Tommy Bailey for helping me with my hives. He came over yesterday afternoon and took both hives apart, teaching me what to look for, and why.

He said the places where the bees had bridged the space between two of the frames was okay for now. We saw eggs, larvae in all different stages, and capped brood where more babies will be hatching. **I watched several babies clamber out of the cells they'd matured in** – that was so absolutely amazing I could have cried.

Look at the places in these first two photos where the bright yellow comb is showing.

The grungy looking brownish junk, shown below here on the inside (bottom) of the lid, is propolis, the glue-like substance that I wrote about earlier this year. The bees had used it to stick the lid to the top of the frames. Thank goodness for my yellow hive tool; otherwise we might never have gotten the lid off.

When it was all over, I brought the super back inside. No comb on it at all yet. I'll put it back in next spring.

BeeAttitude for Day #317: *Blessed are those who keep going in spite of discouragement, for they shall be pleasantly surprised.*

Fran's bee.s. Thank you to those who emailed me asking about the bee sting on my leg. It's still pretty swollen. To get an idea of the size of it, spread your fingers really wide and lay your hand along the side of your leg. I've started taking an antihistamine. Probably should have done that as soon as it happened. *I'll see if I can take a picture of it tomorrow.*

BeesKnees #4: A Beekeeping Memoir

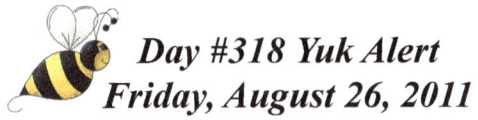

Day #318 Yuk Alert
Friday, August 26, 2011

Yuk notice: if you're squeamish, you may want to pass on this picture.

I promised you I'd show you the bee sting results. Why, you may ask, would I continue bee keeping when this is what happens? Well, since the sting happened when I was in my front yard, I'm going to assume it was one of the wild bees.

My girls are sort of honey colored, which is pretty appropriate for a bee, wouldn't you say? Every so often, though, I see some almost completely black honeybees foraging around the flowers out front.

Since I never did see the bee that stung me, I can think whatever I want to about her identity, right?

Okay, here's the ghastly picture coming up . . . close your browser if you don't want to see it!

Although the swelling's gone down quite a bit, you can still see the big bulge on the right. *No, that is not the way my leg is normally shaped…*

BeeAttitude for Day #318: *Blessed are those who check up on their friends, for they shall help to prevent the dread blog-loss disorder!!!!!*

THANK YOU, PETIE, FOR EMAILING ME. I'D FORGOTTEN TO PUSH THE RIGHT BUTTON

Day #319 Bees are Easier than Cats or Dogs
Saturday, August 27, 2011

I spent Thursday night visiting a friend in north Georgia. On the way back from there I stopped off at Quigley's Rare Books and Antiques on the square in Dahlonega GA, where I signed some books and talked with folks. *[2019 Note: Although my books weren't antiques (not yet!), Quigley's was always generous about selling my books – right across the aisle from a first edition of Gone With the Wind! Like so many small businesses, Quigley's closed some years ago. I was so sorry to see them go.]*

As I left Quigley's, having stayed an hour longer than I'd originally planned to stay, I was quite aware of how easy beekeeping is. I didn't have to clean any litter boxes for them before I left. I didn't have to worry about what would happen if I didn't get back in time to feed them more sugar water. They'd get by even if I'd decided to stay an extra night.

And, thank goodness I never have to take my bees for a walk. Can you imagine 60,000 teenyweeny leashes?

BeeAttitude for Day #319: *Blessed are those who welcome friends into their lives, for they shall be enriched in so many blessed ways.*

 ***Day #320 Bees at the Chicago Airport***
Sunday, August 28, 2011

This is a fabulous idea! Honeybees work the land that surrounds O'Hare Field in Chicago. All that land that an airport needs, but doesn't really use, can be put to good use, and I found a little video that shows how. Google "Bees at O'Hare Field." That should get you there.

I went further, though, and checked out the www.beelovebuzz.com site the beekeeper mentioned. Here's some info I copied from their "about us" page: *[2019 Note: This website has changed considerably since I first wrote this post, but the information is still essentially the same.]*

— Sweet Beginnings, LLC makes the family of beeline® products, an all natural line of raw honey and honey-infused body care products. We extract our honey from our all natural urban apiary in the heart of the North Lawndale community in Chicago. Our honey is known for its complex flavor, a result of the varied flora of our urban environment. Our beeline® skin care products are of exceptional quality and are all unique in their use of the natural gift of honey as a moisturizer. Not only do we respect the earth in the production of our products, but we also provide important transitional job opportunities for area residents who struggle with barriers to employment.

The page goes on to explain the skills the workers learn. It's pretty impressive:
— Sweet Beginnings … offers fulltime transitional jobs for formerly incarcerated individuals and others with significant barriers to employment in a green industry – the production and sales of all natural skin care products featuring its own urban honey. Sweet Beginnings workers care for the bees and hives, harvest honey, make beeline® products, package and ship products, track inventory, fill product orders, and sell at retail outlets and special events. These training and work experience modalities transfer to market positions in manufacturing, food service, distribution, warehousing, hospitality, customer service, and more.

The truly important point here is that "The recidivism rate for former

Sweet Beginnings employees is below 4%, compared to the national average of 65% and the Illinois average of 55%."

Amazing what bees can do—as long as they are partnered with people who care enough to implement such programs.

I love finding proof that bees can make a real difference.

BeeAttitude for Day #320: *Blessed are those who recognize our value and help to increase our numbers, for they shall have honey everlasting.*

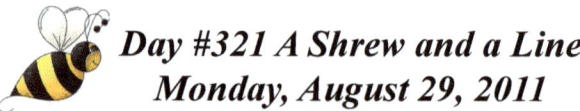

Day #321 A Shrew and a Line
Monday, August 29, 2011

In the past few weeks I've seen two marvelous theater productions, and I'd like to share my delight with you.

The first was *The Taming of the Shrew* at the Atlanta Shakespeare Tavern (shakespearetavern.com). *Shrew* is one of those shows that a lot of people hate in our politically correct times. I've seen it produced many different ways. That's one of the beauties of Shakespeare – you can take the very same words, change the intonation, and get diametrically opposing interpretations.

This production turned out to be raucous, hilarious, and one of the finest love stories I've seen in a long time. I hope you'll check it out. Through the end of September, they're playing it in repertory with *Two Gentlemen of Verona* and *A Comedy of Errors* (which happens to be one of my favorites).

Then, on Sunday I saw *A Chorus Line* at the Aurora Theater in Lawrenceville. First, I must say I'm in absolute awe of anyone who can dance that long and that hard, and make it look that effortless. I was almost reluctant to see it—I'd seen the movie and quite frankly was bored silly. But the play was something altogether different. Beautifully cast, and quite well performed.

Then I came home to my bees and watched their daily production, choreographed by a master planner. Lovely.

BeeAttitude for Day #321: *Blessed are those who work to excel at their craft, whatever it may bee, for they shall be blessed with applause (or with honey).*

Day #322 Dewitt Jones and his celebration of life
Tuesday, August 30, 2011

Dewitt Jones is a photographer who likes to share his work with me (and the umpty-kazillion other people who subscribe to his website). Every so often I get an email with a lovely photograph, some words of wisdom, and a gentle reminder to
"celebrate what's right with the world."

That's a great idea. **I celebrate:**
every time I step onto my deck to listen to the bees,
every time I look out the window at my beehives or the birds,
every time I share time with a friend, and
particularly every time I hear from one of you,
as well as a lot of other times in between.

[2019 Note: Dewitt did a TED Talk that's fabulous. Check it out!**]**

BeeAttitude for Day #322: *Blessed are those who share beauty, for it shall reflect back on them as well.*

Fran Stewart

Day #323 Nighttime Cleanup Crew
Wednesday, August 31, 2011

Birdfeeders are messy. All around them, birds scatter seeds, feathers, and the end products of digestion. That's what they do in my front yard. It's okay, though. I have a cleanup crew who come around every night, 24/7. They never take a day off. They never complain. They keep the area under my "squirrel proof" birdfeeders looking (relatively) tidy.

And I don't have to pay them!

Last night I went out to bring in the feeders—because if I don't, the cleaner uppers climb the pole and empty them for me—and heard scrabblings up the trunk on the majestic tulip poplar that stands near my front door.

I stood still and waited. Within seconds a black-masked little face peeked around the trunk about ten feet off the ground. Before I could say, "Good evening, little friend," a second face poked its way over the first one's shoulder.

Two nights ago, I remembered after I was practically asleep that I'd forgotten to bring in the feeders. I barged out the front door without thinking and startled a possum on my front porch. She cleans up the thistle seeds the goldfinches drop.

During the day, pigeons and doves and other sorts of ground feeders pick up what the raccoons and the possums miss.

And the daddy longleg spiders inside the house clear up any ants that find their way inside.

Life is good.

BeeAttitude for Day #323: *Blessed are those who take the time to observe what we animals do and who appreciate us, for they shall reap the benefit of our activity.*

Day #324 Will Your Dog Be in My Next Book?
Wednesday August 31, 2011

Get Your Dog's Name in My Next Book!

From now through the end of September, anyone who donates $10 to WAG, also known as the *Walton Animal Guild*, will be entered in a raffle. If you win, you can send me a picture of your dog, and I'll use the name, size, breed, coloring, and personality in *Violet as an Amethyst*, my sixth *Biscuit McKee mystery*. Your dog will be a feature character in the plot, and will have his or her bio at the end of the book, along with a photo if you have one available.

[2019 Note: I've deleted the various links in this post because, obviously, the raffle is long over.]

Even if your dog has passed on to greener pastures, you can still enter, and the author's note above your dog's bio will say that this book is "in loving memory of _____"

Naturally, there will be something about bees in this upcoming book, and Marmalade, the orange and white tabby cat, will put in her two cents' worth as she meets the dog.

WAG is a 501(c)(3) rescue organization in Walton County GA.

BeeAttitude for Day #324: *Blessed are those who laugh a lot, for they shall tickle their own hearts when they do.*

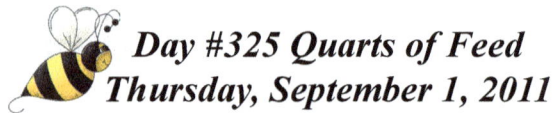
Day #325 Quarts of Feed
Thursday, September 1, 2011

My bees have been eating a quart of sugar water each day now for a couple of weeks. I—who used to avoid the grocery store sugar aisle for the most part—now am buying ten pounds of sugar a week. Do you know how much that costs? I used to spend most of my budget on birdseed. Now it's on bee-feed!

The woman at the checkout lane has eyed me up and down a couple of times. Maybe I should explain to her that the sugar is not for me.

Yesterday one of my neighbors stopped by to thank me for the honey I'd given her. "The best honey we've ever tasted," she said. "My daughter never used to eat honey. She said it never tasted good, but she sure does like this!"

I guess the speaker at last month's Beekeepers Club meeting was right when he said, "Give your neighbors honey, even if it didn't come from your own bees. Just buy it from a good local honey producer. They'll love you for it." I followed his advice.

BeeAttitude for Day #325: *Blessed are those who give from the heart, for they shall find their heart expanding to encompass the world.*

BeesKnees #4: A Beekeeping Memoir

Day #326 An Evening with Frannie
Friday, September 2, 2011

If you've been reading this blog for any length of time, you'll know I don't have a TV set. No entertainment center. No fancy furniture.

Ah! But I have Netflix, and I play the DVDs on an old outdated computer with a monitor that's only about **that** wide – if I sit close enough I can see what's going on.

I also have a sliding glass door that goes out onto my deck where the beehives are. When I watch a movie in the evening, the light from the room (I always have the overhead lights on while I'm watching a movie – can't stand a darkened room with a glaring screen, even if it is only a little one), that light attracts stray bees to the sliding glass door.

And somehow or other a few of them are getting inside. Last night (Thursday), this is how it went:

About thirty minutes into the movie I heard a bzzzbzzzbzzz. A bee, about four feet from my head, was walking up the curtain. I hit *pause*, picked up the plastic container I keep on the coffee table for just this purpose, placed it over the bee, and slid a piece of paper underneath the jar, being careful not to trap the bee's little feet in the process.

"Bzzzbzzzzbzzzzzz," she said.

"I know, I know, I'll get you back outside."

I went to the door, slid the curtain back, and saw about forty bees on the outside. Hmmm. If I open this door to put this ONE bee OUTSIDE, about TWENTY of these other bees will get INSIDE.

So, balancing the bee container, being careful to keep the paper firmly over it, I went to the FRONT door, slipped on my wellington boots (I am not going outside in the middle of the dark night in sandals!), and walked the bee all the way around the house to the back deck, up the stairs and over to the hives. Not knowing which hive the bee came from, I lifted the paper off right between the two hives. I figured she could find her way home from there.

Back around the house and inside. Take off boots. Resume movie.

"Bzzzbzzzbzzz."

This time, the bee was walking across the floor. Jar, paper, boots, around, let go, back around, boots off, movie.

"Bzzzbzzzbzzz." This time, before I went out the front door I turned off the overhead light in the family room. I finished the movie (*Freedom Writers* – very good story, by the way) with no further interbzzzruptions.

Wish me luck figuring out how they're getting inside...

BeeAttitude for Day #326: *Blessed are those who avoid toxic poisons in their yards, for they shall have their plants pollinated by us.*

BeesKnees #4: A Beekeeping Memoir

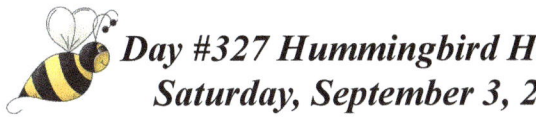
Day #327 Hummingbird Heaven
Saturday, September 3, 2011

Sure I put out sugar water for the hummingbirds, but I really enjoy having flowers they can drink from, too

A couple of days ago I took these two photos with my funny little Nokia phone camera, so you could see the flowering vines that wind up and around my front porch. I love the feathery leaves, and am absolutely amazed that these vines are flowering enthusiastically while everything else in the yard is gasping for water.

The white flowers are from the pokeweed. Yes, I suppose it is a weed, but the birds like the purply blue fruit it produces. Thoreau said something about a weed being a plant whose purpose hasn't yet been determined, and I agree with him, although I tend to think that weeds are highly successful plants that will grow where hothouse varieties won't.

The really grainy-looking photo below was taken through my front screen door. When I moved into this house seven years ago, I replaced all the screening with a heavy duty pet screen, so the cats couldn't accidentally fall out the windows if they leaned against the screens. Unfortunately, pet screen is pretty obvious in a picture.

There WAS a hummingbird there when I whipped out the camera, but of course he flitted off before I pushed the button. Oh well. I'm sure you can imagine him hovering there, sipping away.

BeeAttitude for Day #327: *Blessed are they who live and let live, for they shall find surprises all around them.*

Day #328 Yellow Hive Yikes!
Monday, September 5, 2011

I'm wearing my bee suit every time I step near the hives now. I know I started out having a nice cup of tea each morning out there on the back deck, but for some reason the bees in the yellow hive have developed
an attitude !

You'd think they'd understand when I bring them sugar water that I'm trying to keep them from starving in these drought conditions.

The brown/white hive is very placid. I pull off the empty feed jar and they simply wait for me to put the new one in place.

But the yellow hive! Good grief! The second I remove the feed jar, thousands of them (well, okay, so it's only dozens of them, or maybe a hundred, but they SOUND like thousands) boil out of the hole where the feeder jar goes. I then have a heck of a time getting the new jar in place without squashing bees. If they'd sit still for a few moments, we wouldn't have this problem.

Sunday morning, two of them landed on my slacks and came inside with me. Fortunately I noticed them before any damage was done, either to them or to me. I walked back outside and they flew off. Whew!

Anyway, here's the difference in the hives. I took the picture from my bay window at about 8:00am. As you can see (despite the fuzziness of the photo), the yellow bees are clustered on the front of their hive. The ones in the other colony are inside sleeping, no doubt.

BeeAttitude for Day #328: *Blessed are those who relax when we fly around, for their lack of fear will not frighten us.*

***Fran's bee.s*:** "Frighten you????? That's easy for you bees to say. You oughta try seeing it from my standpoint! Why do you think I'm wearing that silly looking suit all the time now?"

bzzzbzzzbzzzbzzzzzzbzzbzzz (translation: We know you're not scared. You're simply being prudent.)

BeesKnees #4: A Beekeeping Memoir

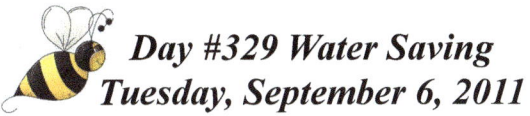 **Day #329 Water Saving**
Tuesday, September 6, 2011

B ees are very aware of water.
They need to drink a lot of it
They have to evaporate a great deal of it from the nectar to form honey
They have to avoid flying in it

I'm aware of water, too. I've been thinking a lot recently about my new bathroom faucet. The good folks at Keep Smiling Plumbing put it in several weeks ago to replace a leaky, yucky iron-deposit-laden mess.

My new faucet even has a name. "Eva." I didn't name it. I think I mentioned a while back that the people who manufacture these Moen faucets name all their plumbing fixtures.

Well, why not? I named my car EllieBug, and the faucet is about the same color as the car (although without the yellow polka dots).

It was hard to turn the old faucet on, and even harder to turn it off. In the middle of this drought that Georgia is experiencing, a leaky faucet is downright irresponsible. Of course, most Americans use WAY too much water. Think about it next time you're getting ready to turn in for the night.

Why do we leave the water running (down the drain and into the sewer or septic tank) while we're brushing our teeth?

Sometimes it's because the doggone faucet is too hard to turn off. But now, I don't ever have to worry about that again.

And all because of Eva . . . They oughta write a song . . .

BeeAttitude for Day #329: *Blessed are those who use water wisely and who make sure we bees have some to drink, for they shall eventually get lots of honey.*

Day #330 Whew! I didn't have to run!
Wednesday, September 7, 2011

Well, it rained all day Monday, so there wasn't a chance to go out and replenish the sugar water on the yellow hive.

I figured there'd be you-know-what to pay when I went out there Tuesday morning. It wasn't raining, but there was a heavy cloud cover, and bees don't like clouds. Plus, because I hadn't fed them the day before, I thought they might be ticked off.

So, I was fairly skitterish when I suited up and walked out there just after noon.

I shouldn't have worried. They looked at me, said "BZZ," which is beetalk for *thank you,* and quietly went about collecting their new sugar syrup windfall.

This just goes to prove
  not everything I read will necessarily apply to my hive, and
  bees don't hold grudges

BeeAttitude for Day #330: *Blessed are those who work though their silly fears, for they shall find relief when they succeed.*

Day #331 The Termites vs. the Bees
Thursday, September 8, 2011

*T*ermites and *Bees*—those sound like opposing football teams, don't they?

All along, since I decided eleven months ago to get a couple of bee hives, I've thought those queen bees were pretty productive—they can lay 1,500 to 2,500 eggs per day for weeks, months, years at a time.

I'm afraid the termite team is going to win this particular game, though. The other evening I watched a documentary I'd found on Netflix that said a termite queen can lay up to 30,000 eggs per day. You read it right – thirty thousand. That leaves my queen bee looking like a slacker.

On the other hand, if a queen bee could lay that many eggs in a day, the hives would have to be ten times bigger than they are. My whole deck would be one enormous hive.

I'll stay with the slow team, thank you.

BeeAttitude for Day #331: *Blessed are those who take life at a (comparatively) leisurely pace, for they still get much accomplished and shall be happier as they do it.*

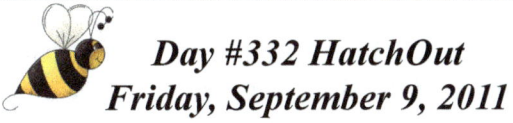

Day #332 HatchOut
Friday, September 9, 2011

Look what happens when a whole slew of baby bees all hatch out on the same day:

On Tuesday I happened to look out the bay window and was, quite frankly terrified, thinking that something awful had happened to my bees. There were thousands of them boiling out of the entrance holes and circling the hives—*both* hives.

I called my mentor, Tommy Bailey, in a panic, but he calmly informed me that since I'd started giving them sugar water three or so weeks ago, the first eggs were all hatching right about now. Remember? the bees were starving and the queens weren't laying any eggs—until I started feeding them.

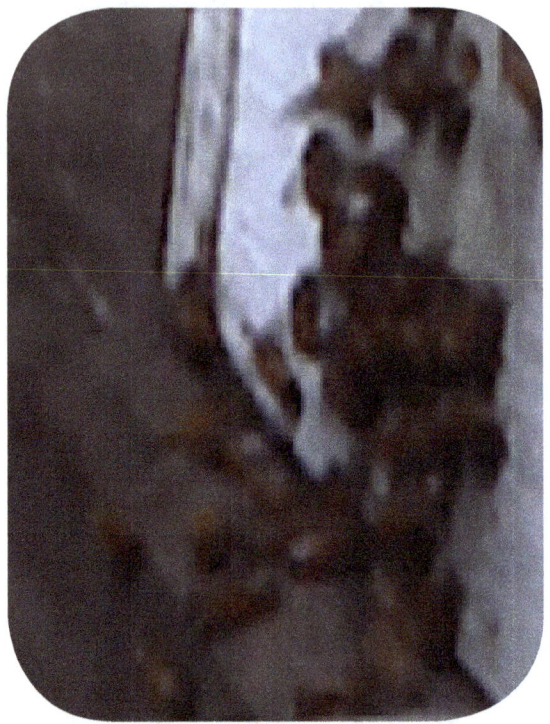

I blogged about feeding them sugar water on Day #311 (Friday, August 19). The queen probably started laying a few eggs at that time, but she really went into production five days later on August 24. How do I know that? Well, as I explained in blog #209, there's a 3612 rule in beekeeping.

$3 + 6 + 12 = 21$.

The brand new egg stays an egg for **3 days**.

Then it hatches into a larva and stays like that, growing constantly, for **6 days**.

Next the nurse bees pack that larval cell with lots of food and cap it over. The larva is now considered a pupa. It stays a pupa for **12 days.**

As soon as a baby bee emerges from her cell, she lets her wings dry a bit, turns around and cleans out the cell she just came out of, and then heads for the front door to take a GPS flight, better known as an orienting flight. That happens **21 days** after the egg was laid.

Voilà! 21 days after that first major egg laying, I saw the **Hatch Out!**

That's when each little bee sets its internal GPS system so it will always recognize home. It only lasted about 15 minutes, and then it was over and everybody settled down to normal. I wonder if there will be another one tomorrow for the eggs she laid just a couple of days later?

Hatchouts occur pretty much every day during the summer, especially when there's been a strong honey flow, but because so many foragers were coming and going from the hive, it never looked like anything special. Little did I know. It took a drought to teach me a bee lesson.

Isn't this amazing?

BeeAttitude for Day #332: *Blessed are those who recognize the small miracles of life, for they shall live in wonder.*

Day #333 A Monkey Wrench in my Spokes
Saturday, September 10, 2011

If you're afraid of bees to begin with, you might want to skip today's post.

I got stung again. Thursday morning, just one sting, on my left hand where the web of skin stretches between the thumb and first finger.

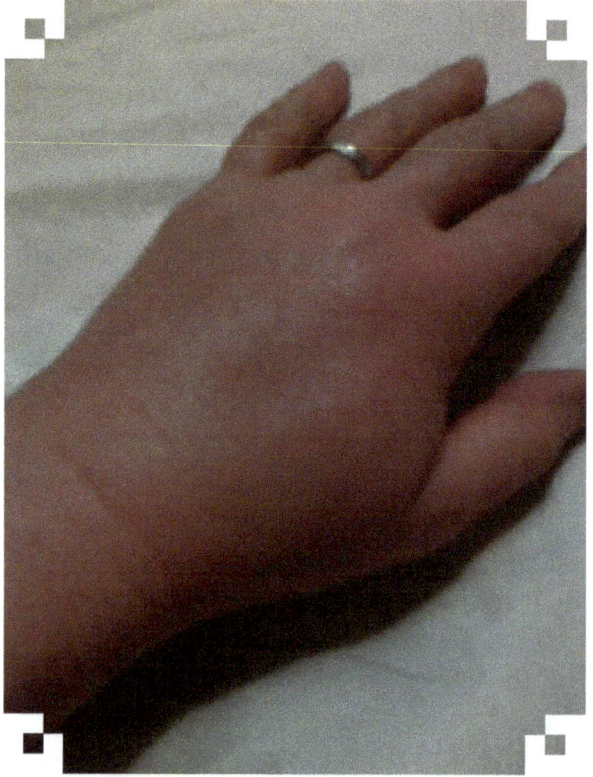

I was ready for it this time. Or so I thought. I came inside, took some Benadryl, and waltzed on through my day. The swelling just keeps spreading; it's two thirds of the way up my arm toward my elbow now. My whole hand, as you can see, looks like a stuffed sausage.

But then, Friday afternoon, one of the hives had eaten its way through the sugar water and needed to be refilled. Did I want a repeat performance? NO.

BeesKnees #4: A Beekeeping Memoir

So I put on three layers everywhere:
>> long sleeved blouse, winter jacket, AND my bee inspector suit
>> two pairs of heavy duty socks and my Wellington boots
>> slacks, sweatpants, AND those huge pants I bought at the Good Will Store

Before I went outside I wrapped a heavy scarf around my hair and topped it with – get this – a quilted, well padded toaster cozy that's patterned after a little English cottage. No, I did not take a picture of myself looking like that! Then I pulled the bee hood over my head and zipped everything up.

Next I pulled on some heavy winter gloves – not easy over my swollen hand AND added my heavy duty leather work gloves.

I looked like a cartoon version of the Michelin Man, but there was NO WAY a stinger was going to get to me.

Once I was ready, I took the fresh jar of sugar water outside, pulled off the empty bottle, replaced it with the full one, waited for the bees to stop flying around me, and came inside where I had to reverse the process. The gloves came off first, followed by the hood and the English cottage toaster hat. And so on.

The good news is that, even if I looked ridiculous, I did not get stung. The good news where my hand is concerned is that, although I can't flex three of the four fingers, I no longer have any wrinkles on that hand. That oughta be worth something...

BeeAttitude for Day #333: *Blessed are those who aren't afraid to look foolish, for they shall open whole new worlds.*

Fran Stewart

Day #334 Epi Pens
Sunday, September 11, 2011

I'd like to use today's post to teach you how to use an epi pen. Ten years ago, a number of very brave people worked around the clock for days trying to rescue as many people as they could from the Twin Towers. I honor those people, and I'd like to do what I can to help you respond to a much smaller scale emergency situation, but one in which you could save a life.

An epi pen is a contraption about the size of a hot dog. Its purpose is to flood the body of a person who is having a severe allergic reaction with *epinephrine*, a drug that speeds up the heart rate and helps to keep the airways open so the person won't suffocate.

Here's what to do:
— If there's anyone else around, holler to them to call 911.
— Open the plastic case and pull out the "hot dog"
— Flip open the blue safety seal on the top of the epi pen
— *Do not touch the bright orange section on the other end. That's where the needle is.*
— Jam the orange end HARD (REALLY HARD) against the front of the patient's thigh to trigger the needle. You can do this right through clothing – even heavy jeans. (Practice it now. Make a fist and **slam** it against your thigh. That's how hard you should jab the epi pen.
— Hold the "hot dog" in place for 10 seconds so the pen can inject the full dose.
— Remove it and gently massage the spot for another 10 seconds.
— If nobody's called 911 yet, you call them now.
— When help arrives, show them the epi pen.

[*2019 Note*: Do not use the epi pen unless the person begins to have trouble breathing. The pen is NOT for just a normal sting or two, which may hurt and may swell a bit. It is for situations in which the throat swells enough to begin cutting off the airways. Then it becomes a true emergency.]

BeeAttitude for Day #334: *Blessed are those who go out of their way to help others, for they shall sleep well at night.*

Fran Stewart

Day #335 Sad News
Monday, September 12, 2011

As you may know, I usually schedule these daily posts to show up at a minute or so after midnight, Eastern time.

I didn't make it today, simply because I couldn't write this last night. I was crying too hard.

I have to give up my bees, and I feel so very sad about this.

The reactions I've had to the bee stings I've received over the past few months have—as I'm sure you can see if you read this blog regularly—become more and more severe.

I can't risk it.

The most recent sting pretty much immobilized my hand—and the swelling made it three fourths of the way up to my elbow. The picture I posted a few days ago was BEFORE it got to the worst point. I realize this doesn't sound very appetizing. I hope you're not eating breakfast while you read this. The swelling was so severe my knuckles are bruised from what little movement I had to make.

Beekeepers get stung. That's just the way it is. I've heard from a lot of my beekeeping colleagues that they get some fairly uncomfortable localized swelling, but they put up with it because, all in all, beekeeping is fun and enjoyable, and the honey it great!

I looked out at my beehives this morning and realized that I'm afraid of those little girls now. As much as I've come to love and respect them (yes, it is possible to love a bee!), I feel that I'm putting my life at risk by continuing this journey. A swollen hand is one thing, but if they sting me on the shoulder or neck, the swelling could close my airway.

As I decide how to end this … this experiment … this journey, I'll keep you informed. You've come this far with me, and I'll feel better knowing I can share the end of it with you.

BeeAttitude for Day #335: *Blessed are those who cry when they need to, for they shall find comfort in their tears.*

Fran Stewart

Day #336 Looking on the Bright Side
Tuesday, September 13, 2011

Thank you to those of you who emailed me (or posted a comment here) about my decision to give up the bees. Your encouragement and understanding have meant a great deal to me.

I'm going to be offering the bees, the hives, and all my equipment (and there's a LOT of it) for sale. I'm thinking of having a "silent auction" sort of affair, where I'll list the stuff and let people jot down how much they'll pay for it.

I guess I hadn't realized how much money I'd plowed into this so far. Well, I did know, because I'm pretty good about budgeting, and I spaced the purchases out so they didn't put a big dent in the checkbook. But I hadn't considered the grand total.

If you're thinking of getting into beekeeping yourself, this is something to keep in mind.

- $ 349   5frame hives (2) with bees (2 deep bodies each)
- $ 4   bee brush
- $ 20   frame perch
- $ 20   hive net
- $ 4   hive tool
- $ 15   smoker (used)
- $ 15   Book: Complete Idiot's Guide to Beekeeping
- $ 6   Book: Honey & Your Health
- $ 10   Book: Honey/Gourmet Medicine
- $ 35   Book: Natural Beekeeping
- $ 35   Education Cards for school programs
- $ 15   Online beginner's class CD from Brushy Mountain
- $ 10   extra veils (used)
- $ 76   Inspector's Jacket w/ zip on veil/from Brushy Mountain
- $ 12   comb cutter
- $ 7   extra honey pail w/ lid
- $ 10   gamma lid

$ 18	glass jars
$ 35	honey filtering system
$ 25	pail holder
$ 20	security tab honey labels
$ 70	5frame supers (7)
$ 40	empty frames
$ 35	plastic frames
$ 886	**Grand Total**

The last 10 items I never really used at all – they all have to do with large harvests of honey but when I look this over I realize I've had more than a thousand dollars worth of fun, and I've had a couple of thousand dollars worth of irreplaceable hands on experience, plus hundreds of dollars of book learning, to say nothing of the new friends I've met through the beekeeping community.

So, all in all, I guess I win!

BeeAttitude for Day #336: *Blessed are those who see the bright side, for their shadows shall always fall behind them.*

Fran Stewart

Day #337
Wednesday, September 14, 2011

Tuesday evening at the meeting for the Beekeepers Club of Gwinnett County, I sold off some of my equipment, and was happy to see it go to people who were enthusiastic about getting it.

The speaker at the meeting, Virginia Webb of MtnHoney (MtnHoney.com) told us about her honey business, and encouraged those of us who would actually be getting honey to be proud to market it.

One thing she pointed out is that local honey is – right from the very start – made in America. Every single product used in beekeeping comes from this country. From the special clothing to the hive components to the bottling equipment to the labels on the jars – all of it is made in the USA.

Honey sold on supermarket shelves (unless it's in a special rack of local honey) is often bottled from "syrup" shipped in from China that is made of 50% processed, heated, pesticide-laden honey and 50% corn syrup.

Not our local honey! Good stuff. Absolutely dependable. Made in the USA.

Be patriotic – buy local honey.

p.s. At the end of the meeting, I taught everyone there how to use an epi pen. You already know how, since you read my blog a few days ago.

BeeAttitude for Day #337: *Blessed are those who appreciate us bees for the work we do, for they shall taste only the best.*

Day #338 It was a Dark and Stormy Night...
Thursday, September 15, 2011

This is so much fun! Dog stuff, I mean.

In two more days the Walton Animal Guild is having an open house to show off their new facility, and I'll be there to talk about *Violet as an Amethyst,* my upcoming book that's going to star one lucky dog.

Would you like a sneak preview? Shh! Don't tell anybody... but here are the first few paragraphs from CHAPTER 1 of Violet as an Amethyst © 2011 Fran Stewart:
= = = = = = = = = =
It *was* a dark and stormy night, dammit, and I was stuck, gasping for air, desperate for warmth, wedged between two branches of a drowning pine tree as the rain swollen Metoochie River tried its river-like best to uproot the nearly submerged tree and drown me. If it didn't freeze me first.

I had no idea who had pushed me from the dock, but I knew I hadn't simply slipped. A moment after I'd sensed I wasn't the only one standing there watching the surge of the storm water, two big hands hit the middle of my back.

What on earth had I been thinking, to take a walk at 2 a.m. when I could have stayed curled up next to Bob? Obviously I'd lost my mind, and now I was paying for it.

I prayed for a convenient lightning bolt to strike the man who'd pushed me, whoever he was. I prayed for dawn. I prayed for a friendly boater or a sudden river drying drought. My only chance was to hang on and hope for rescue. I screamed for help again and again, but heard no answer above the roar of the river. Visions of Snoopy, pounding away at his typewriter on top of his red roofed cartoon doghouse, careened around inside my muddled head. It was a dark and stormy night; it was a dark and stormy night. I couldn't get beyond that first stupid sentence.
= = = = = = = = = =

Doesn't that sound like fun? I couldn't resist starting the book with a cliché, but tweaking it slightly, with the "dammit," so it wasn't totally a cliché. Wait'll you read the end! … um … and the middle, too.

What does this have to do with bees? Well, Biscuit's husband, Bob, the town cop, gets talked into taking over some hives that belonged to a newly deceased town member. But then, there's this dead body that … *Shh, Frannie! Don't give that away.*

BeeAttitude for Day #338: *Blessed are those who anticipate good things, for they shall be eternally hopeful.*

Day #339 Beekeeping at the Fair
Friday, September 16, 2011

The Gwinnett County Fair started Thursday, and a whole slew of folks from our beekeepers club were there to talk to folks about the value of bees. We sold some honey, and I had great fun explaining why the honey came in three different shades. The lightest in color came from the sourwood trees. Then we had a medium toned wildflower honey. The one I'll be buying when I work there next week is the dark, luscious sumac honey.

Then there were the booths just down the aisle from us. Tempting! Geri and I each bought a hat at one booth and a purse at another one. But then we went right back to talk about the bees.

It was fun watching children try to find the queen bee in the two observation hives. Sure, the queens each had a white dot of paint on their backs, but even more than that, you could see the circle of "attendant bees" cleaning them, feeding them, massaging their long backs. The women who were watching invariably said, "I wish I were a queen bee," UNTIL I told them that the queen never leaves the hive and has to lay up to 2,500 eggs every day all spring and summer.

So, come on over and see us at the fair!

BeeAttitude for Day #339: *Blessed are those who explore new options, for they shall be endlessly entertained.*

Fran Stewart

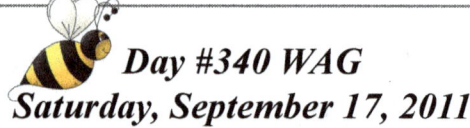
Day #340 WAG
Saturday, September 17, 2011

If you missed the open house at WAG's new office yesterday evening, you missed a good time indeed.

Lots of people showed up to see the little house, to eat yummy food, and to hear a reading from *Violet as an Amethyst*. I read the scene where Glaze and Biscuit see the lost dog for the first time and talked about how I could change it depending on which dog won the drawing.

Of course, people were showing me pictures of their dogs right and left. "This dog would be the best, don't you think?" I had to spread my hands in an "it's not up to me" gesture. Naturally, I'd like it if all the dogs could win.

WAG (Walton Animal Guild) rescues animals from the county shelter and finds homes for them, primarily through showing them at the Logansville PetSmart. It was a day without too much bee activity in my life. I was centered on dogs and my books.

BUT – before I drove all the way to Loganville, I had to be sure my bees had food, so I dressed up in my Michelin Man outfit – four heavy layers everywhere, including the toaster cover over my head under the bee veil. I took this picture of my reflection in the sliding glass door. You can just see the toaster cover behind the screen of the bee veil.

BeesKnees #4: A Beekeeping Memoir

Quit laughing. Oh, what the heck, go ahead. I'm laughing right along with you.

BeeAttitude for Day #340: *Blessed are those who don't mind looking foolish, for they shall find themselves in all sorts of adventures.*

Day #341 A Humbling Experience
Sunday, September 18, 2011

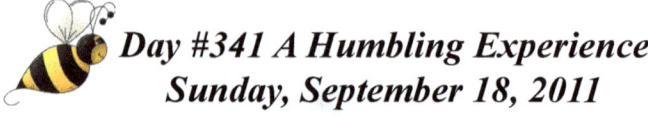

This is a very long post — much longer than usual, but I think it's worth reading. This is the exam given to all eighth grade students in Washington State in 1910.

I had to think twice about some of the answers to the very first question, to say nothing of a LOT of the rest of them. See how you do . . .

==========

OFFICE OF SUPERINTENDENT OF PUBLIC INSTRUCTION,
STATE OF WASHINGTON,
OLYMPIA, WASHINGTON
MY DEAR SUPERINTENDENT AND TEACHERS:

Herewith are sent lists of questions to be used by pupils of the Eighth Grade, who are candidates for certificates of graduation. The aim of these questions is to give the pupils of the Eighth Grade a test in both the technical and general knowledge which they should possess in order to be ready for the higher work. . . .

If a pupil succeeds in passing successfully this test, he will receive a certificate of graduation, and will be entitled to enter upon a high school course. . . .

The papers are to be graded by the county Board of Education. The standard is uniform for the state, and is as follows:

Minimum	60%
Minimum in grammar and arithmetic	80%
Average	80%

Very truly,
HENRY B. DEWEY
Superintendent of Public Instruction

EIGHTH GRADE EXAMINATION QUESTIONS
AUGUST 18 AND 19, 1910

READING CIRCLE WORK
Write a brief review of one reading circle book.

GRAMMAR

— Write the plural of the following words: daisy, leaf, tooth, penny, die, me, tongs, valley, Miss Jones, Mr. Brown.
— Name the four kinds of sentences as to use, and the three kinds of sentences as to structure.
— Give sentences containing noun, adjective, and adverbial clauses.
— Name four kinds of pronouns and give examples of each kind.
— In what must a pronoun agree with its antecedent? Illustrate.
— He felt the damp of the river fog, that rises after the sun goes down. Diagram or analyze.
— Compare: little, much, near, old, up, honest, elegant, famous, neat, merciful.
— Write a sentence containing a verb in the active voice, change it to the passive, and explain how this is done.
— Name three different ways in which a noun may be used in the nominative case, and three ways in which a noun may be used in the objective case.
— Write a letter to a friend describing briefly the country surrounding your home.

ORTHOGRAPHY (*spelling*)

soldier
sustenance
grandeur
obedience
numeral
cancellation
cuticle
declension
buffalo
military
decrepit
irregular
meridian
accurate

phrasing
pernicious
prairie
laudanum
reservoir
beneficent
Manhattan
senator
biography
registrar
emblematic
January
genuine
soliloquy
Siberia
Tuesday

— Write sentences showing the correct use of the following words: beat, beet; great, grate; lain, lane; seam, seem; the, thee.
— Mark diacritically the vowels in the following: banana, admire, golden, ticket, lunch.
— Form words using the following affixes and tell of the meaning of the words thus formed: ary, less, er, ous, dom.
— Define the following words and give examples: primitive word, compound word, vowel, accent, prefix.

UNITED STATES HISTORY AND CIVICS

— What were the three objective points of the Federal forces in the Civil War?
— Name the last three presidents in order, and name an important event in each administration.
— How did the Colonies of the North and South differ as to social life, education, industries, and customs, prior to the Revolution?
— (a) State briefly the causes of the War of 1812.

— (b) Name two engagements.

— (c) Two prominent American Commanders.

— Give a short sketch of the life and work of one of the following great men: Thomas Jefferson, Henry Clay, William McKinley.

— (a) When and where was slavery introduced into America?

— (b) How was it abolished?

— What has made the names of each of the following historical? Alexander Hamilton, U.S. Grant, Harriet Beecher Stowe, Cyrus W. Field, Clara Barton.

— (a) State the qualifications of a United States Senator.

— (b) Name the Senators from the State of Washington.

— How do you distinguish between the terms Puritans, Pilgrims, and Separatists?

— Give an account of the framing and adoption of the Declaration of Independence.

GEOGRAPHY

— What causes the difference in climate between Eastern and Western Washington?

— Name ten wild animals of Africa.

— Tell some reasons why the people of Washington are interested in the Orient.

— Name the five chief nations of Europe, and give their capitals.

— Name five important cities and five products of Canada.

— Sketch a map of South America, locating three rivers, five capital cities.

— What and where are the following? Liverpool, Panama, Suez, Ural, Liberia, Quebec, Pikes Peak, Yosemite, Danube, San Diego.

— Name five of the principal crops of the United States, and tell the section where each is raised.

— Describe the Nile and the country through which it flows.

— Name the largest country of Asia, three important cities, and three important products.

ARITHMETIC
— Divide 304487 by 931.
— Find the sum of 5/9, 5/6, 3/4, 11/36.
— A gardener sells his celery for 8 1/3 cents per bunch. How many bunches should he give for $5.00?
— How many board feet in a piece of timber 14 inches square, and 12 feet long?
— What number diminished by 33 1/3 percent of itself, equals 38?
— By selling my horse for $156 I gained 8 1/3 %. How much did the horse cost me?
— A note for $200 was given January 1, 1909, rate of interest to be 8%. How much was due April 1, 1910?
— Find the square root of 95.6484.
— What is the cost of enough lumber to floor a room 24 feet long and 16 feet wide, at $32 per thousand feet?
— How much will it cost me to pave a street 42 feet wide, and 625 feet long, at $11.65 per square yard?

READING
— One selection in prose and one in poetry from eighth grade reading book. (50 credits) (*not included*)
— Name five American poets, and give a quotation from each.
— Who wrote the following? The Village Blacksmith. Rip Van Winkle. The First Snowfall. The Great Stone Face. The Raven.
— Quote two stanzas of "America."
— Quote a stanza from one of the poems mentioned in question 7.
— Give in your own words the meaning of the following:
"To him who, in the love of Nature, holds
Communion with her visible forms, she speaks
A various language: for his gayer hours
She has a voice of gladness, and a smile
Into his darker musings with a mild

> And healing sympathy, that steals away
> Their sharpness ere he is aware."

PHYSIOLOGY
— Describe the structure of the skin.
— Locate the thoracic duct.
— Trace a drop of blood from the time it enters the left ventricle, until it returns to its starting point, and name the different valves and principal arteries and veins through which it passes.
— Describe the composition of the blood.
— Why are the arteries more protected than the veins?
— Name five special senses.
— Explain why health depends largely upon habit.
— Explain the effect of alcohol and tobacco upon the action of the heart.
— Give some good reasons why boys should not smoke cigarettes.
— What do you understand about the germ theory of disease?

GENERAL QUESTIONS
(Note—Examiners will grade penmanship of pupils from their answers to the following questions)
— Write your name in full.
— What is your age?
— Write your post office address, number of your school district, and name of your teacher.
— To what grade of the school do you belong? Have you completed the grade?
— Is this your first eighth grade examination?
— If you succeed in obtaining an eighth grade diploma, do you expect to attend school next term? Where?

==========

I have to admit it – I'm truly humbled by the breadth and depth of this exam.

BeeAttitude for Day #341: *Blessed are those who expand their minds, for they shall find new worlds in there.*

Fran Stewart

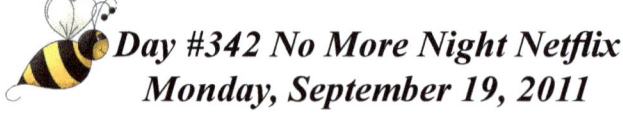
Day #342 No More Night Netflix
Monday, September 19, 2011

I've made a decision. From now on, when I watch a Netflix movie, it's going to be when it's light outside. Thank goodness I don't have a 9 to 5 job! I'd hate to miss my movies.

Why am I doing this? I thought you'd never ask.

Yesterday evening, in the middle of *Les Choristes/The Chorus,* a delightful French film (with English subtitles, of course), I had two interruptions. The first one was great fun—a neighbor to whom I'd loaned Diana Gabaldon's *Outlander* stopped by to return it and to tell me that she'd stayed up till 4 a.m. finishing it. A person after my own heart!

The next interruption, though, was not appreciated. Another bee got through my sliding glass door somehow or other. I think there must be a teeny hole down at the bottom where the door rests on the metal slider thing. I stuffed in a piece of paper towel just in case as a temporary stopgap measure, hit the pause button with my mouse, and scooted to the kitchen to grab the plastic container I use for trapping bees inside the house.

By the time I got back to the family room, the bee was not only NOT on the sliding glass door where had been, but she was NOT buzzing. A quiet bee is a bee that can easily be sat on or stepped on or brushed against. With this bee sting allergy I've developed, I can no longer afford a casual encounter like that.

I kept the container in my hand, checked out my chair VERY CAREFULLY, and resumed the movie, ears attuned to any faint buzzing sounds. Just as the action was escalating in *The Chorus,* there went the bee, buzzleing away inside the ceiling light fixture.

I managed to corral her and get her outside without any problems, but I'm faced with this problem of bees at night, attracted to the light from my family room shining through the curtain on the slider. If another one finds the hole (wherever it is), I might not be so fortunate next time. The last thing I want is to sit on a bee!

So—the logical conclusion is that I keep the light in that room turned off at night. This isn't a problem, since the room is relatively unused—except for my old Netflix movies!!!!! I can't give them up!!!!! Not having a TV set, or anything even vaguely approaching a home entertainment center, I put an old, outdated computer off to one side in the family room, and use it to play the DVDs once a week or so.

From now on, I plan to switch *writing in the morning* and *watching a movie at night*. Not a big deal.

And if it keeps the bees outside where they belong, it's a darn good solution, wouldn't you say?

BeeAttitude for Day #342: *Blessed are those who help keep us bees from getting confused, for they shall learn how to adapt happily to an ever changing environment.*

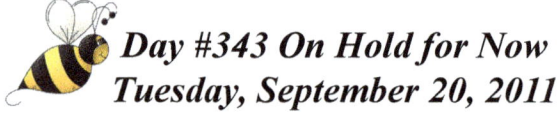 Day #343 On Hold for Now
Tuesday, September 20, 2011

Once when I was traveling back to Atlanta after visiting my sister in Colorado, our plane ended up stuck in between a snowstorm behind us and an ice storm ahead of us.

Nobody was taking off, and nobody was landing; we couldn't go forward, and we couldn't turn back; which meant – there we were circling around. I don't know about the pilot, but I was truly hoping we wouldn't run out of gas.

And now, I feel like I'm in another holding pattern. The bees are doing just great, going about their beely duties. I'm the one who's running around in circles.

I spoke with Rob Alexander a few days ago. He's the one who handles the bees at Rancho Alegré, so he's the one who will end up caring for my bees once they're off my deck. Rob runs 8-frame hives, and mine (as you well know) are 5-frames. So Rob said he'd switch my bees around and organize them into 8-frame units.

Will the bees like that? I dunno.

Bees are fairly adaptable, but this late in the season, they won't have a lot of time before winter to store up honey reserves.

Are my bees going to be okay? I certainly hope so.

Time will tell.

Meanwhile, I'm just circling, waiting for the Gwinnett County Fair to end so Rob will have time to pick up my beehives. Hope I don't run out of gas…

BeeAttitude for Day #343: *Blessed are those who invent new words (like beely), for they shall at least have a good laugh.*

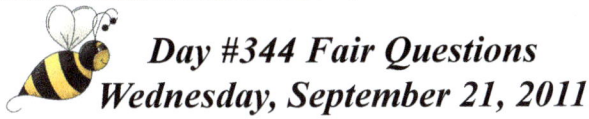
Day #344 Fair Questions
Wednesday, September 21, 2011

I worked the Beekeepers Club booth at the Gwinnett County Fair yesterday from 4:00 till 8:00. Answered a WHOLE LOT of questions about honeybees.

The queen bees in the two observation hives were quite cooperative, flouncing around where the children who visited the exhibit could find them easily. The white dot of paint on their thoraxes helped!

There were quite a few questions about the value of local honey. For the purposes of alleviating allergies, honey that comes from within 50 miles of where you live is considered "local." That is to say, the pollen and nectar from plants within such a radius are likely to have the sorts of properties you need to prevent or lessen allergies.

So, if you're anywhere near the Gwinnett County Fairgrounds, come on by the beekeepers' booth and buy yourself some honey from our good local bees. If you're not going to make it to our fair, then find yourself a local farmers market—there's bound to be good honey there.

Right now, there's a biscuit with my name on it – and some good comb honey to spread on it ... Yum!

BeeAttitude for Day #344: *Blessed are those who support their local farmers, for we bees shall benefit from the success of those farmers.*

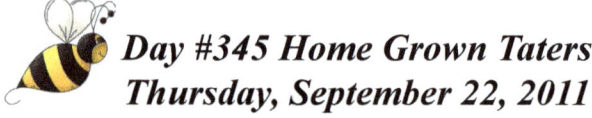
Day #345 Home Grown Taters
Thursday, September 22, 2011

Remember way back this past March (Day #157) when I planted those seed potatoes in an old plastic garbage can on my back deck?

It worked! The plants grew up over the summer (and probably were pollinated by my own bees). Well, harvest time has come. I just scrubbed off a few, and I'm planning to cook them for dinner tonight.

I thought you'd like to see what they look like. They're not very big—that's my blue ringed cereal bowl.

Are they just taters like any other taters? On the one hand, I guess I'd have to say yes. They're like any other good organic potato I could buy at a farmer's market.

But on the other hand, they're mine, and that makes them special. I had fun planting them and watching them grow and harvesting them. Now I'll have fun eating them.

Bet they're gonna taste delicious!

BeeAttitude for Day #345: *Blessed are those who relish the goodness of the earth, for they shall be constantly gratified.*

Day #346 Bees Don't Like Rain
Friday, September 23, 2011

Bee don't like rain, but I sure do.

I have a condition called *vitiligo*, which simply means that I don't have a lot of melanin in my skin. Melanin is the stuff that darkens the skin and protects the body from ultraviolet rays.

It started when I was pregnant with my first child – more than three decades ago. A little white patch appeared over my left eye. Over the following months, the patches spread. At one point my arm looked "like a map of the Alaskan archipelago" – that's what my highly artistic sister said.

Now, all these years later, I simply look extra pale. In the official photographs of the Gwinnett Choral Guild, I'm the one who looks like a ghost.

I don't mind it. But boy do I enjoy rainy days! There is something so relaxing about clouds, lots of clouds. No need to worry about sunburn. It's wonderful!

Now that I have bees, though, I worry about my bees getting wet. What is it about people that we always seem to need to find something to worry about?

BeeAttitude for Day #346: *Blessed are those who accept life's ups and downs, for they shall enjoy the rollercoaster.*

Day #347 Cindy's Weight Loss Idea
Saturday, September 24, 2011

It's time for a laugh or two, folks. This post has nothing to do with bees.

My dear friend, Cindy Pitts Gilbert, owns The Singin' Bean, a coffee house and eatery in Lawrenceville GA. They do karaoke, too, which is where the *Singin'* part of the name comes in. The Bean is where I go when I'm stuck on a chapter. I get a big Crock o' Choc, sit overlooking the intersection of Pike and Perry Streets, and somehow or other the writing begins to flow. Maybe it's all that hot chocolate! I've composed a few of my blog posts there, too. [**2019 Note**: The Bean closed its doors several years ago. Now Cindy (often known as Sister Knowitall) has a **regular online presence,** with her SisterKnowItAll Facebook page. Check her out!]

At any rate, Cindy came up with the best weight loss idea I've ever heard. She said to feel free to forward it. This BeesKnees blog is about as forward a place as I can get.

Here it is, in Cindy's own words:
= = = = = = = = = =
I always wondered what my problem was. Just found out why I am overweight! The shampoo I use in the shower that runs down my body says *"For extra volume and body."*

I'm going to start using dish washing liquid. It says *"Dissolves fat that is otherwise difficult to remove!"*
= = = = = = = = = =
Thanks, Cindy.

BeeAttitude for Day #347: *Blessed are those who disseminate vital information, for they shall feel good about themselves.*

p.s. from Fran – I finally got around to watching (and crying my way through) *Tuesdays with Morrie*. I love Netflix! I'm always about 2 years behind everybody else in what movies I watch, but if I find one I like, I can simply watch it twice.

Fran Stewart

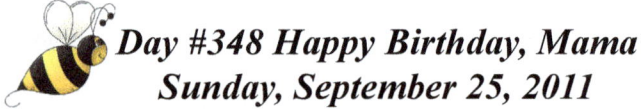

Day #348 Happy Birthday, Mama
Sunday, September 25, 2011

In yesterday's p.s. I mentioned that I'd watched *Tuesdays with Morrie*. The movie seemed particularly apt, simply because today would have been my mother's ninety-ninth birthday if she had lived a few years longer. One of the things Morrie said was that he'd never really had compassion for his father, never saw his pain, never knew what his father was up against.

He could have been talking about me and my relationship with my mom.

I spent a lot of years in anger, resentment, frustration, stuffing all those negative emotions inside – because in my house, it didn't feel safe to express what we really thought.

Now, all these years later, I can connect with what Morrie said. I know now that a great deal of my anger could have been transmuted with a large dose of compassion. Thank goodness I healed my anger before she died.

Someone emailed me the other day saying, "You must be so angry that you're allergic to bees." That's nothing to get angry about. I feel some sadness—well, okay, a lot of sadness—about having to give my bee hives away, but can't see any sense in being angry about my body's reaction to bee stings, something over which I have no control.

I had no control over my mother's depression, either. After all these years, I'm truly sorry she had so much pain in her life. She was doing the best she could. I can feel compassion for her.

I'm also going to treat myself with a bit more compassion. Sure, I held in that anger for way too long. But I, too, was doing the best I could.

My sister, Diana Alishouse, created a series of fabric art pieces that show what depression feels like. Her book, *Depression Visible: The Ragged Edge* shows what someone who is bipolar experiences. I never understood either my sister or our mother until I read Diana's book.

Morrie said, "Forgive everybody everything."

Where was Morrie forty years ago when we needed him?

[**2019 Note:** This year I took over publishing her book through my new publishing company, My Own Ship Press. She added a quilt (and a chapter) called *PTSD*. Be sure you look for the 2nd edition. It's the one with that new chapter.

BeeAttitude for Day #348: *Blessed are those who let go of the dross, for they shall fly unencumbered.*

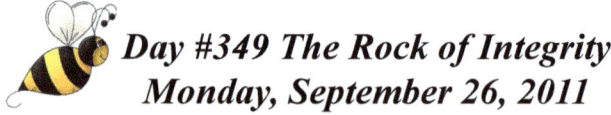
Day #349 The Rock of Integrity
Monday, September 26, 2011

Before I forget – my friend Cindy emailed me to thank me for including her in that funny "weight loss" post – but she said she hadn't come up with the idea. It was something she found somewhere or other on Facebook and simply reposted.

As a writer, I always appreciate being credited with what I've actually written, but the Internet has made dissemination of disinformation so incredibly easy. It's tempting to say, "Oh, who cares?" After all, it's not the end of the world if I say Cindy came up with the shampoo/dish detergent idea when it was really So and So from somewhere or other who first wrote it.

No. It's not the end of the world. But it is one little fragment flaked away from the rock of integrity. The more often we chip away at that rock, the smaller it will become.

I've wondered over the past week, working occasionally at the Gwinnett Beekeepers booth at the fair, whether I should even claim to be a beekeeper anymore. After all, in another week or so I won't have any hives on my back deck. When I've discussed bees with people ogling the observation hives, trying to spot the queen, I've been selective about who I've mentioned my allergy to. To most of them, I've simply said that I'm a hobbyist beekeeper with two hives on my back deck and that I love my 60,000 girls. Which is *technically* true.

Is there a similarity between crediting the wrong person for a funny story on Facebook and acting like a beekeeper when I'm not one anymore?

I'm not sure of the answer to that.

All I know is that, with the printed word at least, I'm going to continue to try my hardest to give credit where credit is due. I'd expect that from people who read and enjoy what I write, and I will certainly be meticulous about how I present other people's writings.

BeesKnees #4: A Beekeeping Memoir

If whoever wrote the shampoo/dish detergent blurb will please contact me—I'd be happy to give you credit for it.

BeeAttitude for Day #349: *Blessed are those who stay in integrity even when it's hard to do, for they shall always find a sturdy rock to sit on when they are tired.*

Fran Stewart

Day #350 Stone Soup
Tuesday, September 27, 2011

I used to subscribe to an eservice called the Daily Om. Each day I'd receive an inspirational email, and I particularly enjoyed this one. Years ago I read the children's book, *Stone Soup* by Marcia Brown, without realizing that it was based on a very old folk tale that seems to have shown up in the oral traditions of many countries.

Here's what the Daily Om said about it. The first paragraph summarizes the story. The second paragraph is what I really want to share with you, though.

= = = = = = = = = =

There are many variations on the story of stone soup, but they all involve a traveler coming into a town beset by famine. The inhabitants try to discourage the traveler from staying, fearing he wants them to give him food. They tell him in no uncertain terms that there's no food anywhere to be found. The traveler explains that he doesn't need any food and that, in fact, he was planning to make a soup to share with all of them. The villagers watch suspiciously as he builds a fire and fills a cauldron with water. With great ceremony, he pulls a stone from a bag, dropping the stone into the pot of water. He sniffs the brew extravagantly and exclaims how delicious stone soup is. As the villagers begin to show interest, he mentions how good the soup would be with just a little cabbage in it. A villager brings out a cabbage to share. This episode repeats itself until the soup has cabbage, carrots, onions, and beets—indeed, a substantial soup that feeds everyone in the village.

This story addresses the human tendency to hoard in times of deprivation. When resources are scarce, we pull back and put all of our energy into self preservation. We isolate ourselves and shut out others. As the story of stone soup reveals, in doing so, we often deprive ourselves and everyone else of a feast. This metaphor plays out beyond the realm of food. We hoard ideas, love, and energy, thinking we will be richer if we keep them to ourselves, when in truth we make the world, and ourselves, poorer whenever we greedily stockpile our reserves. The traveler was able to see that the villagers were holding back, and he had the genius to draw them out and inspire them to give, thus creating a spread that none of them could have created alone.

= = = = = = = = = =

I have to admit, I've always thought that this was what really happened with the loaves and the fishes—people were drawn out of their self-centered hording, and all were fed with plenty left over. And *that* is a miracle indeed.

This is what the bees do. They make enough honey for themselves, but then they keep right on producing. It's the excess honey, honey the hive doesn't need but creates anyway, that beekeepers take. I'm going to think about that the next time I spread honey on my biscuits. And I'm planning to share the honey I'll get from my hives.

I'll be getting that honey because Rob Alexander, who could easily have kept every bit of honey from those hives of mine that he'll be tending at Rancho Alegre, told me he'd give me back half of the excess honey they produce. My own sweet Stone Soup.

BeeAttitude for Day #350: *Blessed are those who share our honey, for they shall have lives filled with sweetness.*

Day #351 Great Big Spider
Wednesday, September 28, 2011

A great big elegant spider of an unknown species (unknown to me, that is) has taken up her residence outside my bay window. Her body is wider than my thumb (and I have fat thumbs!). I took these two pictures of her against the reflections from the window. This first (fuzzy) picture shows her size. The second (fuzzy) one shows her legs. The orange in the background comes from the early morning lights inside as the spider ran toward the side of her web.

The other day, she ate one of my bees.

I have to admit, I was a bit ticked off at her. I rather like spiders. They eat lots of bugs. In fact, I imported some daddy longlegs a while back so they could eat up the itsybitsy ants that had invaded my kitchen.

But eating one of my bees was going too far. She wrapped the hapless bee in a graceful silken sack and hovered over it for quite some time. I think she was sucking out all the juices. Yuck!

Today, though, she's back to eating mosquitoes and aphids. Hope she stays away from the bees from now on.

I've decided to assume that the bee she ate was at the end of its six week life cycle. That's recycling at its best.

BeeAttitude for Day #351: *Blessed are those who recycle, for they shall have a cleaner world. (But we bees wish they wouldn't recycle us too early!)*

Fran Stewart

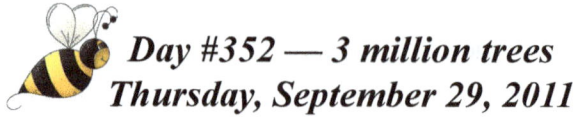

Day #352 — 3 million trees
Thursday, September 29, 2011

Krista Tippett, a public radio host, interviewed Wangari Maathai in 2006, and I was fortunate to have heard a rebroadcast two years ago. In introducing the program, which Tippett called *Planting the Future,* Tippett said:

==========

She is a biologist by training, in her late 60s, with flashing black eyes and a presence that fills the room. Wangari Maathai received the 2004 Nobel Peace Prize. Sitting across from her, it is not hard to imagine that this woman stood up to a dictator and won, and that she's fought off encroaching desert by planting 30 million trees. Wangari Maathai knows what many in the West have forgotten: that ecological crises are often the hidden root cause of war.

For a quarter century, she battled powerful economic forces and Kenya's tyrannical ruler, Daniel arap Moi. She was beaten and imprisoned, but her Green Belt Movement has now spread to 600 communities and into 20 countries. "The Earth was naked," Wangari Maathai has said. "For me, the mission was to try to cover it with green."

Caption: *Wangari Maathai of Kenya holds her Nobel Peace Prize in the Oslo City Hall, Norway, on Dec. 10, 2004. The first African woman re-*

cipient of the Nobel Peace Prize has died after a long battle with cancer, it was announced Monday. (Bjorn Sigurdson, Pool/Associated Press)

Wangari Maathai died earlier this week at the age of only 71, and a Nairobi twitter post about her death said, "No wonder the sun is not shining today." That's quite an epitaph.

==========

At the fair last week, I had a lot of children ask me what happened to honeybees when they died. The sun keeps on shining when a bee dies, but—in their small way—every bee in a hive counts. Some of those 30,000,000 trees that Wangari's force of women planted, assuming a number of them are fruit trees, most likely depend on bees for pollination. Those trees will grow stronger and healthier, not only because of Wangari Maathai, but also because of bees.

BeeAttitude for Day #352: *Blessed are those who find something in life to be passionate about, for their enthusiasm shall enrich their lives and those of others.*

Fran Stewart

Day #353 Goodbye to Another Favorite
Friday, September 30, 2011

This seems to be the week for dying. First a bee, then Wangari Maathai, and now one of my favorite stores.

I found GrainsnMore through Rancho Alegre, the place where I buy goat milk, meat, fresh produce, all of it organic and delicious. GrainsnMore was one of the locally owned businesses that distributed products through Rancho Alegre.

I bragged about GrainsnMore on Day #282. That's where I bought my wonderful Teeccino, which brightens my teacup every morning (and afternoon and evening) with its perky –and non-caffeinated – taste. And coconut oil. Vanilla beans. Steelcut oatmeal. All of it organic and wholesome.

Several days ago I received a call from Dan, the owner, telling me that they couldn't fill my latest order for two more bags of Teeccino, because they'd had to close down. Not enough orders to avoid the steadily increasing shipping costs from his suppliers, costs that he couldn't pass on to his customers.

For bees, the cost of doing business is reflected in the high early mortality rate when they are subjected to herbicides and pesticides. At least Dan and his wife still have life. They're bright and intelligent, and I have no doubt that they will get through this rough time. They'll figure out what to do to make it.

Bees don't have that option. They gather nectar, trusting that it will be good, not knowing that some ill-informed soul, in quest of the *"perfect"* lawn, has sprayed RoundUp on stray weeds (which just happen to be blooming, inviting bees for a sip).

BeeAttitude for Day #353: *Blessed are those who support local businesses by buying from them regularly, for they shall find open doors wherever they go.*

Fran Stewart

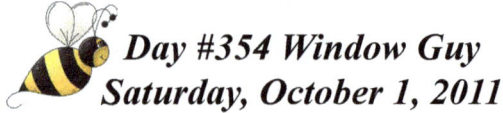
Day #354 Window Guy
Saturday, October 1, 2011

The Hollander family in Youngstown, Ohio runs the nicest window company, and I'd like to brag about them. A few days ago I received an astonishing phone call from them. I'll need to give you a little background, though.

While I was working at the beekeepers booth at the Gwinnett County Fair, I took a little break to walk around and see the other exhibits. One of them was for Weather Tite Windows. I stopped for a moment and spoke with a young man named Sam. I told him I was in a hurry to get back to the honeybee booth, but that I'd try to stop by later. He was nice enough to bring me a brochure.

I told him about a harrowing experience I'd had when someone from another company came to give me an estimate. That guy was HORRIBLE! Pushy, pushy, pushy! I finally had to ask him to leave my house. And I complained to the company, but never received any sort of apology from them. "If you send somebody like that," I told Sam, "I'll be very upset with you."

"No, ma'am," he said. "All our people are really nice, and we depend on the quality of our product to sell itself." He told me a few more things about the company—there weren't any visitors at the bee booth right then—and I signed up to receive a call so we could schedule an estimate.

The lady who called the next day was as pleasant as could be. And the fellow who came to show me their windows and give me an estimate was downright likeable. I ended up telling him that I would do business with them, although I had to get a few more royalty checks before I could schedule the work. I don't believe in paying by credit. I save up for what I plan to buy.

A couple of days later, when I was back working at the fair, I stopped by the Weather Tite booth again and told the young woman what a pleasant time I'd had dealing with their company. I mentioned Sam specifically, and Jim Wall, the estimator.

The next day, Aaron O'Brien, the president of Weather Tite Windows, called me to thank me for such positive feedback. It brought to mind something that happened when I was in line at Publix on 9/28. The woman in front of me asked if she could write her check for $200 (about $18 over what she had bought). When the clerk handed her the change, she accidentally handed back the check as well, underneath the bills. The woman returned the check, *and the clerk seemed surprised at that.* Why would anyone be surprised by honesty? Shouldn't fairness be automatic? Shouldn't *acting honorably* be the norm?

In an economy such as we're experiencing now, it must be tempting to go for the hard sell, to rake in the customers, to push a more expensive window when someone doesn't need it. Weather Tite doesn't do any of that.

I'd be willing to bet they hire only nice people.

And I'll let you know as soon as I get my new windows. I'm pretty sure it's going to be a good experience.

[**2019 Note:** I tried to reach Weather Tite a few months ago because one of my windowpanes is cracked and needs to be replaced. Not only do they not have a Georgia representative now, but the woman I spoke with in Ohio said she couldn't help me since I'm *out of state*. I put a long strip of masking tape over the crack and keep that particular window covered with a curtain. Not a problem since that the window is where the cats have their flap so they can access the screened porch.]

BeeAttitude for Day #354: *Blessed are those who act with courtesy and consideration, for they shall sleep soundly at night.*

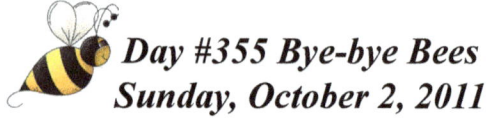
Day #355 Bye-bye Bees
Sunday, October 2, 2011

Yesterday morning, Rob and Tommy came by to take my bees to their new home.

I cried.

I also tried to give Rob the bee box brander I'd bought from Brand New, "because," I said, "I'm not a beekeeper anymore."

"Yes, you are," he told me. "You still have the bees; they're just going to be living somewhere else."

The transfer was easy (except for my crying) in part because the weather has turned quite cool. At 10:30 in the morning, it was only about 48 degrees Fahrenheit / 9 degrees Celsius, so almost every single bee was inside the hive.

In fact, when Rob and Tommy each picked up a hive, they were both surprised at how heavy they were. That's good news. It means the bees have been making good use of the supplemental feed I've been giving them, and they should have enough honey to get them through the winter, particularly since their new home will be in the middle of fifty acres that right now are filled with goldenrod, and my bees will have several weeks for harvesting. Goldenrod honey is good honey.

I still won't get any honey until next spring, but that's okay. My bees got off to such a slow start, I'm just glad they survived. Rob kept reassuring me yesterday that the hives were strong now and should make it through the winter just fine.

Here the hives are, loaded on the back of the truck. You can see where the guys stapled screening over the entrance holes.

And this next photo was my last view of the hives, as Rob backed his truck out of my driveway.

If you've read this blog for any length of time, you've seen lots of pictures of the hives, taken through my bay window. The scene looks awfully empty now, with that slash of dark shadow from the deck railing looking like a slash across the whole enterprise. And no, that is not paper trash all over the deck. Loads of autumn leaves look white in the bright sunlight.

There are about a dozen bees flying around the concrete blocks where their hives used to be. Rob said they'd figure out another place to go, possibly find a wild hive they could join. With their little gifts of pollen-filled corbiculae, I imagine they'd be welcome anywhere.

As I try to type this Saturday afternoon, through my tears I see an enormous Pileated Woodpecker land on one of the nearby trees in my back yard. Life goes on.

BeeAttitude for Day #355: *Blessed are those who keep their eyes open, for they shall see wonders the rest of the world misses.*

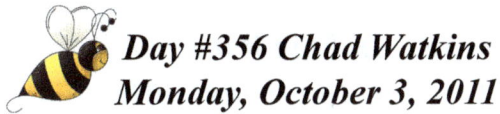
Day #356 Chad Watkins
Monday, October 3, 2011

Piano music – real piano music, not the fake synthesizer stuff – has always been a favorite of mine.

Last week the most beautiful music was playing during my reflexology session. Of course, I asked Jan, the reflexologist, what the CD was. It's called *The Journey*, written and performed by Chad Watkins (www.chadwatkins.com).

So I ordered a CD for myself.

I'll be playing it a lot, I think, now that the bees are gone. I need something to make up for their happy buzzing.

BeeAttitude for Day #356: *Blessed are those who create music, for their hearts shall always sing.*

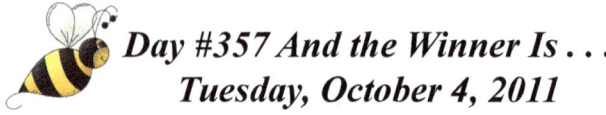# Day #357 And the Winner Is . . .
Tuesday, October 4, 2011

Here's another post that has nothing to do with bees.

For the past month you've been putting up with those dog announcements at the bottom of my posts *[2019 Note: I removed most of those when I was reformatting this into book form]*, and many of you, from Colorado to Michigan to Florida to Scotland (!) and lots of places in between, responded by contributing to the Walton Animal Guild. I wish all of you could have won, but there's room for only one new dog in my next book.

Three years ago, Gracie was rescued by Carol and Ted Baum from the parking lot of a drugstore, where she had installed herself as the official outside greeter, apparently looking for just the right people to adopt. They took her to an animal shelter so her original owners might find her. When she wasn't claimed, Carol and Ted went right back and brought her home. She was in pretty bad shape physically, but with lots of love and good vet care, Gracie rebounded to good health.

I love happy stories.

So now, Gracie will grace the pages of *Violet as an Amethyst, the sixth Biscuit McKee mystery*. I'm having great fun working on rewriting the dog scenes to incorporate Gracie's color and size AND that fluffy tail. I'll be sure to let you know when it's released (both print and e-book).

BeeAttitude for Day #357: *Blessed are those who care enough to give animals a home, for we shall repay them with love (from the dogs, cats, and horses) and with honey (from the bees!)*

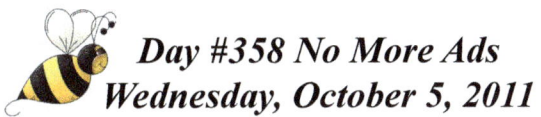
Day #358 No More Ads
Wednesday, October 5, 2011

You might notice that I've removed all those ads from my blog site.

I got to thinking about ads in general. I don't have a TV set—in large part because 20 or so years ago the commercials began to irritate me so much I decided to take them out of my life. There were other things I objected to, like the vacuous look on the faces of people (probably myself included) as we watched whatever was on the set, and the amount of time I found myself wasting watching shows that may have been entertaining, but that, in the long run, simply didn't enrich my life. Still, it was the commercials that grated on my nerves the most.

I know we all buy things, and I know that advertising a business is important for the business owner, but somehow or other, I don't want any more to be a part of bombarding people with ads. If I find a good business that I enjoy dealing with, I'll brag about it here and in conversations with friends. I won't, however, allow any more ads on this site.

I started the ads because of a hype-filled Google campaign that said something like, "Let your blog pay for itself!" Here's just one of the blurbs they put forth:

> [imagine oversized, colorful Google and Blogger logos here}
> Free, simple way for Blogger users to earn money by displaying targeted Google ads on their blog.

I'll admit, that sounded like a good idea. Every time you opened one of the ads, I got a few cents. And there was an option that allowed me to block certain types of ads:
>   get rich quick,
>   fast weight loss,
>   religion,
>   politics,
>   cosmetic surgery,

enhancing youknowwhat,
and so on.

But what I found was that you were, for the most part, uninterested in the ads. How do I know that? After 350 days of this blogging, the ads had earned me only $55.21.

I don't regret having removed the ads from this blog site. The rotten thing about it is that Google now has $55.21 in my "AdSense" account, but their proviso was that they'd send me a check whenever the balance reached $100.

Now that I'm out of the program, do you think they'll send me the money?

I won't hold my breath waiting for it.

I hope you appreciate the change. It cost me $55.21 to make it...

BeeAttitude for Day #358: *Blessed are those who plant flowers that bloom in the autumn, for we bees shall sing for them as we gather fall nectar.*

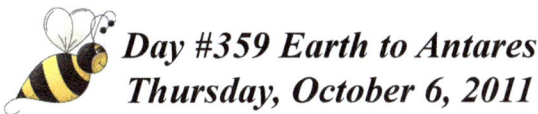
Day #359 Earth to Antares
Thursday, October 6, 2011

Someone sent me one of *those* emails recently. You know the ones I mean. They're characterized by: ENORMOUS fonts, usually in a bolded bright red, along with a *shake-their-finger-in-my-face* narrative that tells me:
    how little I understand,
    how little I can think for myself,
    how ungrateful I am for all the riches life offers,
    and what horrible things will happen if I don't forward the message immediately.

I hate those emails.

Every once in a while, though, one shows up that has something interesting in it. And I steal those ideas for my blog.

The email I have in mind had a series of pictures of various sized balls. The first showed a teeny Pluto, a slightly larger Mercury, a bigger Mars, a still larger Venus, and a great big Earth.

In the next picture, Earth was dwarfed by Neptune, and the sizes moved progressively up through Uranus and Saturn to an enormous Jupiter.

In the 3rd picture, Jupiter was miniscule compared to the Sun.

In the 4th, the sun, Sirius, and Pollux, each in greatly increasing sizes, were nevertheless insignificant when compared to Arcturus.

And of course, Arcturus wasn't even a 100th the size of Betelgeuse, which was about half the diameter of Antares.

Antares, incidentally, is more than a thousand light years away from earth, barely a hairsbreadth away when one considers the limitless span of the Universe.

The email ended by telling me that I ought to feel horribly humble in the face of all this HUGENESS (that's my word, not the email's).

On the other hand, miniscule fleas caused the Plague that devastated Europe, killing the major bulk of the population, and the great big people were powerless to do anything about it.

People may be able to grow to be six or seven feet in height, while a honeybee never reaches much more than about half an inch or so, yet the honeybee is responsible for pollinating 1/3 of our food products. Without all those teeny bees, we'd be in deep doodoo.

Relative size has very little to do with relative importance. I think we all have our role to fill, whether we are a bee, a planet, a star, or a person who sends emails. And it is what we do with our lives here and now that gives us value—not how little we are, or how big either.

BeeAttitude for Day #359: *Blessed are those who take themselves with a grain of salt, for they shall enjoy a flavorful life.*

Day #360 The Spider Again
Friday, October 7, 2011

Remember how I kept telling you I wanted to get a good picture of that spider I talked about a week or so ago? I took a good enough picture of her so you could see her relative size, but then I forgot about it. So this picture makes it look like I still have hives on my deck, even though they've been gone for almost a week.

Thank goodness I don't have my bees here anymore to feed her enormous belly.

Of course, I hope you realize that this picture, taken from my bay window, distorts the relative sizes. The spider's tummy is NOT the 6inch diameter it appears to be!

The good news, though, is that while my bees were here, they must have attracted a number of wild honeybees to my yard. I went out to the mailbox Wednesday and found hoards of bees on the wild asters beside my driveway. I've lived in this house for seven years or so, and I've never seen this many bees around in the fall.

Fran Stewart

I know you can't see them in this picture from my crummy little phone camera, but you can, I'm sure, imagine them buzzing away in complete disregard of me and my mailbox errand.

BeeAttitude for Day #360: *Blessed are those who let the wild native plants grow, for they shall receive beauty where they least expect it.*

Day #361 Weather-stripping for Bees
Saturday, October 8, 2011

Remember climbing those pine trees when you were a kid? Remember coming home all streaked with sticky sap?

Bees are experts at gathering plant resins (sticky sap), turning it into something called propolis, and using it to weather-strip their homes. Why? I'm glad you asked. Bees are masters at climate control, and wayward drafts mess up their ability to monitor the temperature and humidity of the hive.

I started out with hives that had screened-over ventilation holes. Guess what? The bees used their sticky propolis to cover each little open square on those screens. I feel bad that I caused them so much extra work.

Misguided beekeepers who think they know better than bees (HA!) have tried for some time to breed a strain of bees that don't produce as much propolis. Now, I don't know how successful they've been at that, but I do know that any such bees would be at a distinct disadvantage coming up on winter.

In the winter, whether bees are in the relatively mild south or the (brrr!) frigid north, one of their biggest enemies is condensation. They need to keep the temperature of the cluster at 96 degrees. When condensation forms on the underside of the hive lid (as happens frequently when people put metal lids on there!) the moisture drips down onto the bees. How would you like to spend the winter with wet skin? The condensation can also form when the bees haven't been able to plug up all the holes and cold air leaks in.

Is your home weather-stripped and ready for winter? If so, you're imitating the honeybee. Isn't that nice to know? I just hope you didn't use tree sap to do the job. Leave that to the bees!

BeeAttitude for Day #361: *Blessed are those who let us bee, for they shall not waste their time in ludicrous pursuits.*

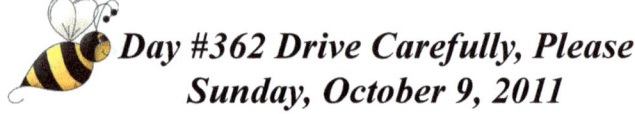 Day #362 Drive Carefully, Please
Sunday, October 9, 2011

I am so embarrassed about this, I can't believe I'm admitting in such a public forum, but I feel compelled to admit—to confess—that I ran a red light Friday.

I'm not talking about scooting through when the orange light has just turned. And I'm not talking about easing into an intersection in the middle of the night when there's no other traffic anywhere in sight.

I'm talking about 35 miles per hour idiocy.

I have no excuse.

Thank God the truck driver who had already entered the intersection hit his brakes. Thank God the sedan halfway through the intersection stomped on the gas to get out of my way.

And double thank God nobody was coming from the right.

I slammed on my brakes, but saw that I couldn't possibly stop in time to prevent myself from ramming the front right fender of the truck, so I veered to the right and swerved around in front of the truck, just missing the back end of that speeding up car.

I made it all the way through the intersection without killing anybody, myself included.

I would have pulled to the side of the road and collapsed, but there wasn't a shoulder to pull onto. So I drove on, made it to my lunch meeting with my editor on time, and managed not to choke on all the what-if statements that zoomed through my head.

I've always prided myself on being a careful, defensive driver. I've never, to my knowledge, caused a wreck.

BeesKnees #4: A Beekeeping Memoir

And still, in those few moments of inattention—whatever was I thinking?—I could have murdered someone. You see, I do believe that the person at fault in a fatal car crash *has* committed murder. The fact that it is without intent simply doesn't excuse the one who is to blame.

So please, please drive carefully. You never know when you might blunder into the path of a driver like me.

BeeAttitude for Day #362: *Blessed are those who own up to their errors and who resolve not to make the same mistake again, for they shall bee a little bit safer than beefore.*

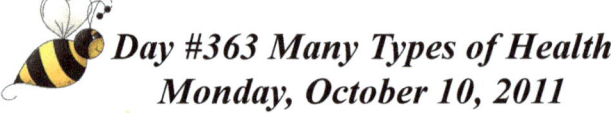# Day #363 Many Types of Health
Monday, October 10, 2011

Health comes in many forms.

For bees, the health of a hive can be determined by how many eggs the queen is laying, and how many of those eggs hatch successfully.

But I'd like to think that hive health is reflected in more poetical terms. When my bees were starving in early August, they weren't singing. The hives were depressingly silent. But as soon as I'd fed them for three or four days, the buzz quotient went WAY up. In short, they were happier, so they sang.

Health is a state of complete physical, mental, and social wellbeing, and not merely the absence of disease or infirmity.
~World Health Organization, 1948

One of the most important factors in a state of vibrant health is the ability to laugh. Petie Ogg, one of the first fans of this blog, sent me this picture of her being "clutched" by *Clutch*, the Houston Rockets mascot, when she participated in the Susan G. Komen Race for the Cure.

Thanks for the chuckle, Pete! Great photo!

And congratulations on your good health.

BeeAttitude for Day #363: *Blessed are those who laugh hard every day, for they shall enjoy the sweetness of life.*

Day #364 Hurry Slower
Tuesday, October 11, 2011

Sometimes, when life is feeling a little bit frantic, it's a good idea to remember how bees handle all the jobs they have to do.

Photo Credit: Ranko Zilic (Pexels .com)

One at a time.

Although every worker bee takes on every single job in the hive, no bee tries to do them all at once. They do this for a day or two and that for a day or two, this job for three days and that job for five.

Photo Credit: Kat Jayne (Pexels .com)

Twelve of them, pooling their efforts over the course of their six-week lives, can make a teaspoon of honey.

And I thought *I* had it hard ...

Photo Credit: David Hablützel (Pexels.com)

BeeAttitude for Day #364: *Blessed are those who take their time, for they shall hurry slower and get everything done in good measure.*

Day #365 Blue Ridge Honey Company
Wednesday, October 12, 2011

Tuesday evening, Bob Binnie spoke at our Gwinnett County Beekeepers meeting. Bob's a commercial beekeeper, who's been in the business since 1981.

He and his wife own the Blue Ridge Honey Company. His talk was fun, informative, and interesting from start to finish. I came home from the meeting and went right to his website.

On his FAQs page, I found all sorts of interesting tidbits that I'll be sharing with you over the next few days.

Here's one: *What is beeswax used for?*
Beeswax is used in candles and ornaments, lip balm, cosmetics and medicinal creams, as foundation for new honeycomb in bee hives, and in sewing to lubricate needles and thread. Beeswax keeps belts in vacuum cleaners, sewing machines, and other tools from slipping. It is used to waterproof shoes, fish line, and clotheslines, to lubricate doors, windows, and tools, on skis, toboggans, and bow strings, in furniture or floor polish, and so much more...

Are you using beeswax without knowing it?

BeeAttitude for Day #365: *Blessed are those who share what they know and who listen when others share, for they shall all increase the wisdom of the hive.*

p.s. from Fran: 365 days???? My gosh, have I really been blogging for an entire year?

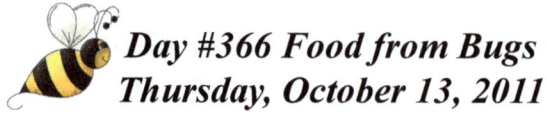
Day #366 Food from Bugs
Thursday, October 13, 2011

In some area of the world, people routinely eat various bugs, such as grasshoppers (I've heard they're pretty tasty when they're fried), ants (covered in chocolate, anyone?), and assorted other six legged critters. But when it comes to the food those bugs eat (such as aphids, plant saps, and dirt), we humans are not interested. Honeybees, though, are the only insects that produce food humans like to eat.

Isn't that worth a little cheer?

Hip-hip-hooray for the honeybees!

BeeAttitude for Day #366: *Blessed are those who live attuned to nature, for they shall sing with the rising sun.*

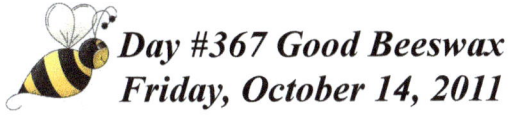

Day #367 Good Beeswax
Friday, October 14, 2011

Here's another little snippet from www.BlueRidgeHoneyCompany.com

Is it okay to eat the beeswax from comb honey?
It has long been believed that honeycomb is good for you in moderation. It is thought to be good for the digestive tract and the blood. Recent studies at the University of Georgia suggest that ingesting as little as one gram of beeswax can help lower cholesterol.

I love eating honeycomb, just a little bit at a time. But please keep in mind that I eat it because it's *good*, not because it's *good for me*.

For years, my voice mail message has ended with the suggestion to "Drink plenty of water, because it's good."

I suppose I'm lucky in that I enjoy many things that also happen to be good for me, but the *enjoying* is, to my way of thinking, more important than the *goodforme* part.

Just for a moment, think about what you enjoy.
>
>
>
>
>
>
>
>
>
>

There! Didn't that feel great?

BeeAttitude for Day #367: *Blessed are those who share what they create, for they shall fuel the imagination of those around them.*

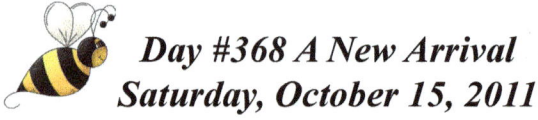

Day #368 A New Arrival
Saturday, October 15, 2011

I got to thinking about bees and honey. Are you surprised by this?

We humans eat the *excess* honey, in the same way that when we drink milk, it's the *extra* milk, the gallons and gallons of it that the calves don't need.

Rancho Alegre, the organic farm in nearby Dacula, has a brand new calf, just a few days old, and the new mom has an abundance of milk.

In the state of Georgia, it's illegal to sell non-pasteurized milk for human consumption. Unpasteurized milk must be labeled "For Pet Consumption Only." I agree that milk produced by huge conglomerates has to be pasteurized for our protection. We have no idea what those cows have been eating or what their living conditions are.

Just as we have no clue, generally, of what supermarket honey contains (things like corn syrup imported from China, where pesticides have killed so many of the natural pollinators that Chinese farmers have to use little paint brushes to hand pollinate their crops).

Photo Credit: P. Quintero 2011

BeesKnees #4: A Beekeeping Memoir

Rancho Alegre is where I buy my locally grown, safe, delicious produce that's been pollinated naturally. I get goat milk there, too. My cat, Miss Polly thrives drinking goat milk. Daisy, my other cat, doesn't care for it. Go figure.

The first one who gets the cow's milk, though, is this little lady in the photo that Pilar Quintero, Rancho's owner, was kind enough to let me use. I love the way the calf's tongue is just barely visible.

And—would you believe it? Her name is VIOLET! If that doesn't ring a bell, you may not know that my upcoming book—due to be released in another month or so—is called VIOLET AS AN AMETHYST. I love coincidences!

Anyway, I just thought you'd like to meet Violet.

Isn't it lovely the way the sun illuminates the veins in her ear?

BeeAttitude for Day #368: *Blessed are those who nurture the little ones, for they shall sleep with a warm feeling in their hearts.*

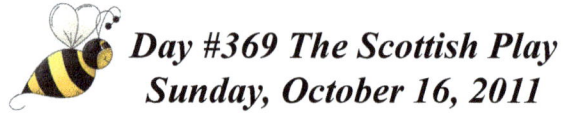
Day #369 The Scottish Play
Sunday, October 16, 2011

I must admit, I was relieved when the three weird sisters in Macbeth chanted around their cauldron Friday night at the Shakespeare Tavern in Atlanta. Despite the many times I've seen that play, parts of it still surprise me.

This year, because bees have been so much on my mind, I was somewhat nervous waiting for the "double, double, toil and trouble" speech. I knew they threw "scale of dragon" and "root of hemlock" into the pot, along with a number of other extremely odious, nasty things, but I couldn't remember—had they thrown in various parts of a bee as well?

I'm happy to report, they didn't. Bee parts would have sweetened their brew, I'm sure, and Shakespeare couldn't have had that happen. Then again, as I've mentioned before, Shakespeare must have been a beekeeper—"To bee or not to bee…"

My two 11-year-old grandchildren were entranced. The porter's silly speech, the sword fights, the sleepwalking scene.

If you've never seen the Scottish Play, as it's called in the superstitious theater world, where speaking the name of that play aloud is considered bad luck, I strongly recommend it. It speaks to this time as powerfully as it did to the Elizabethans. The corrupting influence of power seems, unfortunately, to be as timeless as Shakespeare's dialogue.

BeeAttitude for Day #369: *Blessed are those who know the sweetness of honeybees, for they shall sing happily in their dreams.*

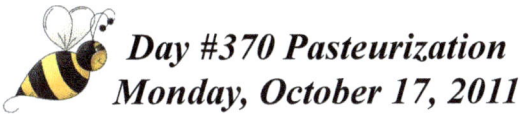 Day #370 Pasteurization
Monday, October 17, 2011

Time for another tip from Blue Ridge Honey Company:

Why not to pasteurize honey:
Honey will deteriorate when exposed to heat. The higher the heat, the faster and greater the effect.

For example, honey has numerous enzymes. Most of these enzymes remain stable under 100°F but have decreased activity when exposed to temperatures over 120°F. For instance, the enzyme diatase, which is common in honey, shows a 50% reduction in activity after 15 days at 122°F. Most enzymes in honey are almost completely destroyed when exposed to temperatures above 160°F for even a short period. These enzymes are also destroyed when honey is liquified in a microwave oven. An interesting side note is that most of the enzymes in honey are added by the bees.

Interestingly enough, they also tell us the reasons in favor of pasteurization:

Why pasteurize honey?
Honey contains yeasts. These yeasts are very different from the yeasts used in bread, vinegar, and alcoholic beverages. They will cause fermentation in honey with a moisture content over 18% to 19%. These yeasts can be killed by heating honey to 160°F for a short duration of time. The heating of honey to high temperatures will also cause a delay or slowing of granulation by the dissolving of small sugar crystals present in raw honey. These crystals can initiate the granulation process. The heating of honey also thins it **so it can be finely filtered**.

I added the bolding of that last sentence. Fine filtering, which many companies subject their honey to, removes a lot of the good elements in honey – little bits of pollen, little bits of wax, little bits of dead bees—protein, anyone?)

BeeAttitude for Day #370: *Blessed are those who live in tune with nature, for they shall rise up with bounteous energy to see the sunrise.*

Fran Stewart

Day #371 To Filter or not to Filter
Tuesday, October 18, 2011

Yesterday we looked at reasons to pasteurize (or not pasteurize) honey. Today, let's draw once more on the wisdom of Bob Bennie at Blue Ridge Honey Company. This is taken from the FAQs page on his website.

Why filter honey?
Honey is commonly filtered to remove sugar crystals, air bubbles, particles of beeswax and pollen, and any other hive debris that may be present. Fine filtering of honey makes the honey bright and clear and removes anything that could act as a platform for sugar crystals to build upon and therefore facilitate the granulation process. Simply put, it gives the honey a longer shelf life without granulation and a better appearance for purchase appeal.

I much prefer the thought of unfiltered honey, though. An awful lot is lost during the filtering process.

Why not filter honey?
The fine filtering of honey removes much of what makes raw honey a healthy and desirable food. This would include particles of pollen, beeswax, and propolis.

Which do you prefer?

BeeAttitude for Day #371: *Blessed are those who sing in the rain, for they shall call green into their lives.*

BeesKnees #4: A Beekeeping Memoir

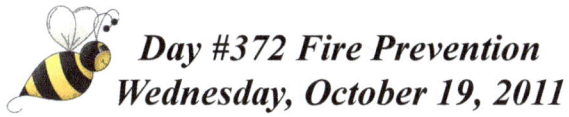
Day #372 Fire Prevention
Wednesday, October 19, 2011

After seeing this picture on Facebook of a firefighter (Jeff Clark) being licked by a dog he'd rescued, I've been thinking about bees and fire.

A smoker supposedly makes bees think fire is in the area. The bees begin to gorge on honey. Beekeepers who know about such things say that the bees are preparing to leave the hive, taking their honey with them. At best, this is a guess. Who knows what bees are thinking?

Still, it seems to me the stress of believing fire is about to consume their home must be awfully hard on the bees.

That's why I tend to agree with those beekeepers who try to keep their hive inspections to a minimum. How would you like it if somebody terrified you on a regular basis, and afterwards always said, "I was just kidding"?

Yeah. That what I'd think too.

And, by the way, the "dog kiss" happened on August 1, 2009. Just goes to show you how long stories can go around and around and around.

BeeAttitude for Day #372: *Blessed are those who do what is kind, for they shall get extra points.*

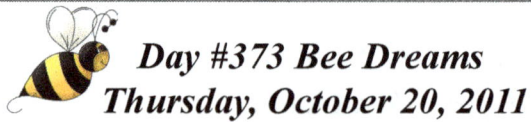

Day #373 Bee Dreams
Thursday, October 20, 2011

My mother lived through the Great Depression. She used to tell me stories about how she would get her hands on a Sears & Roebuck catalog, and go through it circling item after item, turning down the page corners to mark especially winsome articles of clothing or particularly striking pieces of household goods. After she'd marked hundreds of dollars worth of purchases, she'd dust her hands off and go back to work.

Eventually the catalog would end up in the outhouse and be put to very good use indeed.

I do that with J. Peterman Company catalogs. Not the outhouse part, but most definitely the turning down of pages. I don't order very often, but ah! the dreaming is magnificent.

On rainy days, like the last few have been here in Georgia, I wonder what the bees dream about. Do they carry in their little bee brains a catalog of winsome tastes in nectars, exquisite varieties of pollen, and the very safest locations for retrieving water?

I hope so.

BeeAttitude for Day #373: *Blessed are those who put foundations under their castles in the air, for they shall sense accomplishment.*

BeesKnees #4: A Beekeeping Memoir

Day #374 Daisy's Hidey Hole
Friday, October 21, 2011

Bees can't fly when their wings are wet, so a long-lasting rainstorm can be something of a disaster for a hive. A bee caught out in a rainstorm must take shelter right away, perhaps under a large leaf or in a handy hole in a tree trunk.

That may be why bees tend to get a bit cranky when the skies cloud over. Do they take the risk of flying out and possibly being trapped by the rain? Do they stay home and bypass a chance to bring in more food for the hive? Decisions, decisions.

Indoor cats never get into such a quandary. One particular indoor cat, though, is fascinated by umbrellas and will sit for half an hour at a time under one that is spread out to dry, even when the human with whom she shares her house lies down on the floor in front of her to take this picture.

BeeAttitude for Day #374: *Blessed are those who make the most of their circumstances, for they shall BEE contented.*

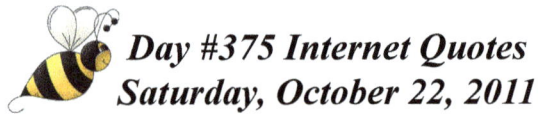

Day #375 Internet Quotes
Saturday, October 22, 2011

Bees never have to worry about the Internet. Lucky bees.

I wasted an inordinate amount of time this morning (before breakfast!) trying to look through the entries on my Facebook site. Some of them are fascinating, some of them are puzzling, and some – the ones I hide – are sheer drivel.

Still, I found some goodies that I'll be sharing with you over the next few days, starting with this little gem that Kathy Barrett Trader posted.

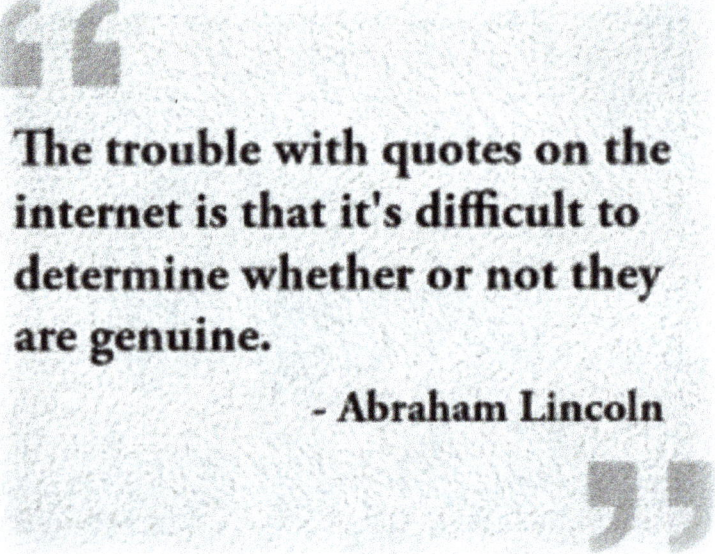

" The trouble with quotes on the internet is that it's difficult to determine whether or not they are genuine.

- Abraham Lincoln "

Makes one think. Not a bad idea.

BeeAttitude for Day #375: *Blessed are those who choose to keep their hearts light, for they shall fly through life like us bees, finding sweetness wherever they alight.*

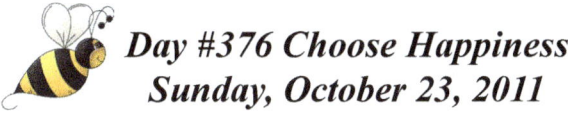

Day #376 Choose Happiness
Sunday, October 23, 2011

Here's another photo gleaned from my hour on Facebook the other day.

It's from "Choose Happiness," and Beth Leeper is the one who posted it.

Choose Happiness. Another good idea.

BeeAttitude for Day #376: *Blessed are those who accept what is while still planning for tomorrow, for their hives shall be filled with sweet honey.*

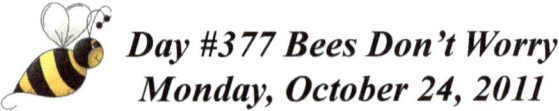
Day #377 Bees Don't Worry
Monday, October 24, 2011

Bees don't worry about holidays, so why do we people? I'd prefer to think that bees celebrate life every single day. Maybe there's a stir through the hive when a new, rich nectar source is discovered, or when a new queen hatches, but I doubt they concern themselves with stringing lights over the shrubbery or bringing dead trees inside.

I pretty much decided to give up on holidays a number of years ago. I found I was stressing out and completely losing the concept of "celebration." I'm not a Grinch. I'm not opposed to the idea of holidays. I simply choose not to buy in to the mania that grips this country from October through the end of December and one day into each New Year.

Since I've been sharing Facebook funnies with you – I couldn't resist this wisdom from Maxine.

BeeAttitude for Day #377: *Blessed are those who take each day with gladness in their hearts, for they shall garner true wealth – "peace it bodes, and love, and quiet life."*

p.s. from Fran. Yes, bees *do* quote Shakespeare, at least in this blog. They like *The Taming of the Shrew* almost as much as I do.

BeesKnees #4: A Beekeeping Memoir

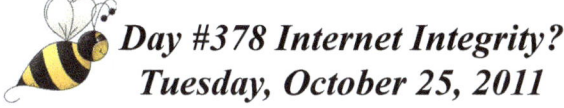
Day #378 Internet Integrity?
Tuesday, October 25, 2011

Bees always tell the truth as they understand it. If there's a good nectar source southwest of the hive, that's the direction they advertise to their hive mates through their waggle dances, which I talked about in a post last November (Day #33). They wouldn't dream of sending their bee friends off on a wasted trip.

Some people, though, send friends in the wrong direction deliberately, and the Internet has made this habit much easier, both for the perpetrators and for the innocent *forwarder*, who doesn't stop to check facts. Here's the reply I wrote to an email that you've probably already seen— the one that says that this October has a highly unusual, so-called "Moneybags" pattern of days. Nonsense!

"I hate to be the Grinch about this," I wrote, and continued:

"but I do wish people would stop forwarding astounding-sounding emails that have no basis in fact whatsoever. I'm appalled that anyone would think the 5 Saturdays, 5 Sundays, and 5 Mondays event "occurs only once every 823 years."

In ANY month with 31 days, whatever days the 1st, 2nd, and 3rd fall on, will always have 5 weeks of those days that month. If the first of the month happens to fall on a Saturday, then the 5 days will occur Saturday, Sunday, and Monday.

In fact, if January 1st falls on a Saturday, then there will TWO months that year with the "Moneybags Pattern"—January and October. If January 1st is a Saturday in a leap year, then the 2nd so-called Moneybag month will be in July.

You really wanted to know all this, didn't you?

There is always at least one and never more than two of these "moneybag" months every year, with the following exception. There is one yearly pattern that contains NO "moneybags."

If January 1st falls on a Tuesday, and the year is not a leap year, then there will be no such pattern. The five most recent examples of this pattern were 1957, 1963, 1974, 1985, 1991, and 2002. The next one coming up will be 2013.

This means that in the last 40 years, there have been 34 that fall into this "moneybag" pattern.

So, if you're looking for an excuse for prosperity, and you believe the calendar holds the key to it, you are blessed indeed to have so many "moneybag years" at your disposal.

Anyone with a perpetual calendar and a little patience can figure this out.

p.s. The abundance in your life is not determined by how many times you forward ANY email. Feel free to break those e-chains!
p.s. #2 Blessed are those who, if they must forward, do so via blind copy, for they shall preserve the integrity of the Internet. (Is that an oxymoron?)

BeeAttitude for Day #378: *Blessed are those who deal honestly, for they shall eventually find that the cards have been stacked in their favor.*

 ## Day #379 Whoever said this had it right
Wednesday, October 26, 2011

I seem to spend an inordinate amount of blog space comparing people to bees.

· If we'd only act like bees we would be better organized.
· If we acted like bees, we would stay more focused.
· If people were more like bees, we'd produce better products.

But then, I found this:

> Everyone is a genius. But if you judge a fish on its ability to climb a tree, it will live its whole life believing that it is stupid.

That's right. People are not bees. We can learn from them, but I shouldn't go judging people on how well they can do their honeybee chores. After all, I'm not too good at gathering nectar myself.

BeeAttitude for Day #379: *Blessed are those who live in the moment, for they shall save themselves from excessive worry.*

Day #380 Monoculture Almonds
Thursday, October 27, 2011

Last night I attended a screening of the documentary *Queen of the Sun*. If you get a chance to see it, please take the time. Gorgeous filming of honeybees, fascinating interviews with beekeepers, entomologists, biophysicists, all of whom have deep concerns about what we're doing to the bees.

I've never before seen a monoculture almond farm – 60,000 acres of nothing but almond trees. Never until this film took a camera in a small plane flying over mile after mile of almond trees in military rows. Those trees bloom for two or three weeks once a year. When they're not blooming, there is NO FOOD on that land for bees. That's why commercial beekeepers from all over the country load up their hives—several hundred at a time—onto flatbed trucks, and haul them to the California almond farms, killing hundreds of thousands of bees as they go.

What on earth, this movie asks, would be wrong with plowing up an acre of land every so often, scattered throughout the almond farm, and planting wildflowers and clover and herbs? Then install some hives on each of those acres. That way, the bees can live year-round in what is now a virtual desert. Those bees will turn it eventually into a vital oasis. Think of the savings to the almond farmers (and all those other current monoculture crops), if they didn't have to pay commercial beekeepers from all across the country to stress out their bees by hauling them 20,000 miles in a season.

It's something to think about.

BeeAttitude for Day #380: *Blessed are those who let us live in a natural environment, for they shall have safe honey in abundance.*

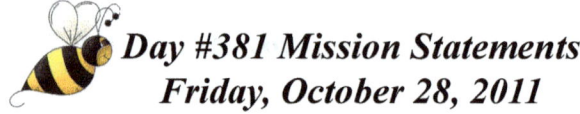
Day #381 Mission Statements
Friday, October 28, 2011

I sing with the Gwinnett Choral Guild, and I'm a member of the Strategic Planning Committee. We've been meeting recently to flesh out our mission and vision statements.

You'd think it wouldn't be that complicated. But what, after all, are we really about? Singing, of course. Musical excellence. Community. How, though, do we craft those essential statements? How do we agree where we are and where we're going?

Bees don't have that problem.
· Mission – honey and pollen.
· Vision – survival of the hive.

Hmmm. I want more than food and survival. And I'm pretty sure the whole GCG will want more than that as well.

So, in this, I guess we people don't have to emulate the bees.

BeeAttitude for Day #381: *Blessed are those who know who and what they are, for they shall rest easy.*

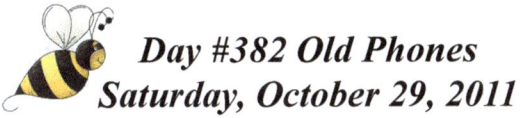
Day #382 Old Phones
Saturday, October 29, 2011

If I'm remembering right, my first phone number, on an Air Force base overseas, was something like 53, or maybe it was 537. The phone was the old, heavy, black, corded, sit on the desk model. And only one phone in the entire house.

Photo Credit Pixabay (Pexels.com)

Then, for a while, I lived in a mountain town in Colorado that had a teeny phone company. That phone number was W5R, or some such crazy combination. Try telling that to a long distance operator.

Now it's all cell phones – and no need to push a 1 before the ten digits.

The story keeps floating around the Internet that cell phone signals mess up the navigation systems of honeybees.

The scientists at the honeybee laboratory at the University of Florida, however, tell us that there's no such problem. Bees apparently blithely ignore cell signals.

Whew! That's good to know. I'd hate to dial W5R and have nobody BEE there.

BeeAttitude for Day #382: *Blessed are those who keep in touch, for they shall live in ever widening circles.*

BeesKnees #4: A Beekeeping Memoir

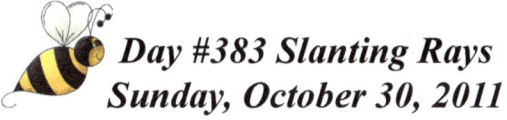 ### Day #383 Slanting Rays
Sunday, October 30, 2011

The late wild asters are still blooming, but they're beginning to get brown around the edges, and some of the blooms have disappeared completely. Very few bees were in evidence today – not surprising, since the temperature has been dipping lower and lower each day.

Still, the sun was bright, and Miss Polly and Daisy snoozed in the afternoon rays slanting in through my bay window. If I'd had a good camera, I might have taken a picture like this one:

I gleaned it from the Internet, of course. You'll have to picture cats rather than dogs.

BeeAttitude for Day #383: *Blessed are those who appreciate sunshine, for they shall have wonderful naps.*

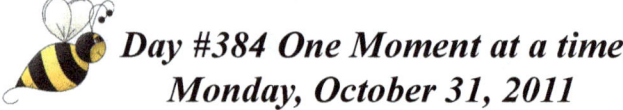
Day #384 One Moment at a time
Monday, October 31, 2011

DeWitt Jones sent out one of his wonderful inspirational photos Sunday, accompanied by this quotation:

The miracle is not to walk on water.
The miracle is to walk on the earth in the present moment,
to appreciate the peace and beauty that are available now.—Thich Nhat Hanh

This is how the bees live. In the moment. Every moment.
We could learn something from them.

BeeAttitude for Day #384: *Blessed are those who listen and see and hear, for they shall know their world.*

Happy Halloween!

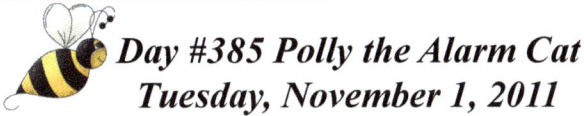 Day #385 Polly the Alarm Cat
Tuesday, November 1, 2011

I've had people ask me why I believe people can hear animals' speech and animals can understand what people are saying.

Here's the story.

A number of years ago, at a time when I had ten or eleven indoor rescued cats living in my house, one of them started peeing in a highly inappropriate place, in the living room. After two days of this, I was fed up. I couldn't catch the culprit in the act.

An animal communicator who lives in California had been highly recommended to me. I called her on Friday and told her what the problem was. She asked me the names of my cats and the hair color and eye color of each of them, as well as their ages and how long they had lived with me. That's all I told her.

She hung up, contacted the cats telepathically, spoke with each of them, called me back, and told me that it was Miss Polly who'd been peeing. "She's trying to get your attention," she said. "Polly is very angry with you because you moved a red furniture."

"What?"

"That's what she told me," Dr. Ryan said. "She said that you had moved a red furniture and she couldn't sit on it to watch the birds out the window anymore."

She was right. I had moved a big red overstuffed chair from my bedroom, where it sat in front of a window, to the middle of the living room. The peeing started the next day, right next to that chair.

I explained that to Dr. Ryan and asked, "Does this mean I can't move my furniture?"

"No, not at all. You're the mom. But Polly would appreciate it if you would tell her before you move anything. Change scares her, and she'd like to know what's going to happen."

"Is she going to stop her peeing?"

"Yes," Dr. Ryan said, "but she would like you to put another chair or a table next to that window so she can watch the birds. And could you move the red chair closer to one of the living room windows?"

"Sure," I said. "Not a problem."

"By the way, Polly told me that she would like to have a regular job."

"A job? For a cat? What kind of job do you give a cat?"

She made soothing noises. "I'm sure you'll think of something."

I mailed off a check to her. That night, I set my Zen alarm clock (which has an amazingly quiet little *ding*) for 6 a.m., since I had to be at an early meeting the following morning. Just before I went to sleep, I turned my head toward Polly, who was, as usual, sleeping next to my pillow, and said, "Polly, would you be sure to wake me up at 6:00 tomorrow morning? I don't want to sleep through the alarm."

The next morning I was in that semiconscious state just before waking. The alarm hadn't gone off yet. As it clicked, a second or two before the first ding, I felt three little pats on my cheek. I opened an eye. Polly's head hung close to my face.

"Thank you, Polly," I said, just as the alarm clock went *ding*, secretly sure that this was just a coincidence.

The next morning, when I might have slept in a bit, 6:00 came with three little pats on my cheek despite the fact that the alarm clock was not set.

The next morning, same thing. And the next. And the one after that.

When daylight savings time switches, we always have a week or so to adjust, and I've finally convinced her that 6:30 is more reasonable that 6:00.

Still, every single morning since then, she has woken me with those three little pats. If I stroke her back a couple of times and mumble "ten more minutes, Polly," she'll go away and come back a little later, sort of like a built-in snooze button. I can do that three times. After the third time, though, she puts her little paw directly onto my eyelid. That's when I get up with no delay.

I asked Dr. Ryan once why I couldn't hear my own cats.

"It's because you aren't *really* willing to hear everything they might tell you."

I think she's right. Maybe that's why I couldn't hear what the bees were saying.

[2019 Note: I wrote about this in WHITE AS ICE the last of my Biscuit McKee books. I figured it was about time everyone knew why Marmalade had been making all those comments over the previous ten books.]

BeeAttitude for Day #385: *Blessed are those who listen well, for they shall be illuminated.*

Happy 11-1-11 !

Day #386 Spiral Arms
Wednesday, November 2, 2011

Astronomers have, according to a posting on NASA Science News, been cataloguing stars for more than 400 years. There are, as Dr. Tony Phillips put it, "dwarf stars, giant stars, dead stars, exploding stars, binary stars; by now, you might suppose that every kind of star in the Milky Way had been seen."

Not so.

Someone found a star with Spiral Arms.

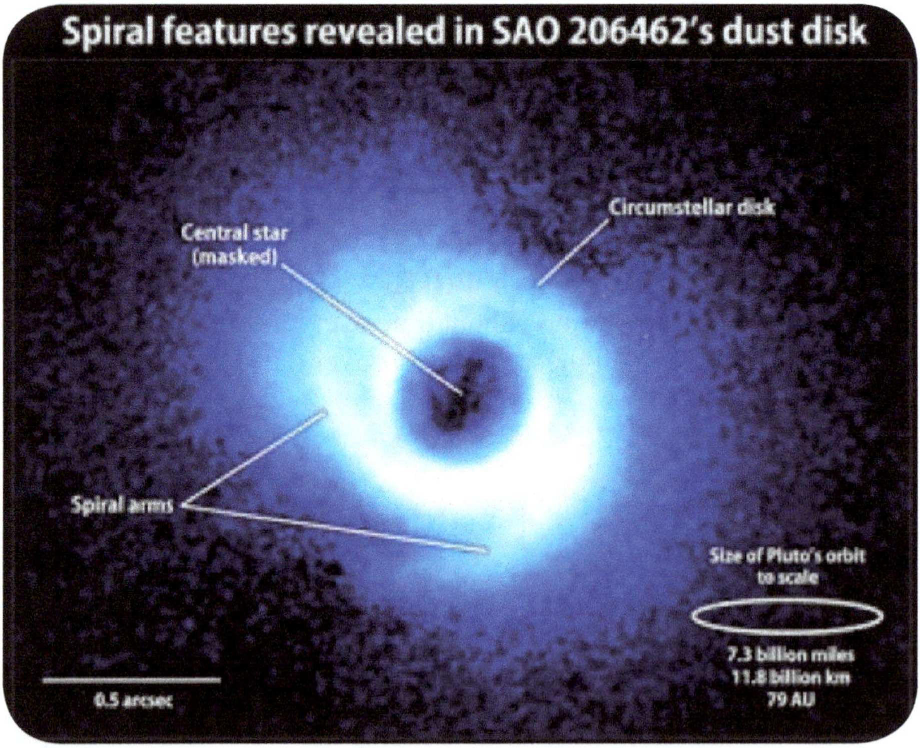

Cool, huh?

It's only 400 light years away from earth. Speaking cosmically that's practically next door.

It stretches more than twice the diameter of the orbit of Pluto. That's big. Really big.

And nobody ever noticed it before.

Don't you wonder what else we don't know, what else we're not even aware of not knowing?

What is there about bees, trees, the ocean, the people around us that we've just never noticed? May we could look a bit closer...

BeeAttitude for Day #386: *Blessed are those who study the stars, for their vistas shall be infinitely large.*

bee.s. and the ones who look at us with kind intent, for they shall bee astounded.

Fran Stewart

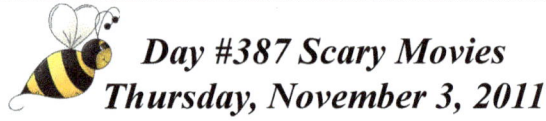

Day #387 Scary Movies
Thursday, November 3, 2011

Do bees ever get scared? Not that I'd have any way of knowing for sure, but I rather think they don't. People, on the other hand, do. Maybe not every person, but the one who's typing this blog post at 2:30 in the morning, certainly.

I have a dear friend who, from the very first episode, was addicted to the *XFiles*. For years I've heard her raving about that show. I finally decided to get my old Netflix in gear and order the first XFiles movie.

Darlene had told me, of course, the general idea of the XFiles being a fight against horrible extraterrestrials who want to take over the Earth. "How bad can that be?" I thought, forgetting that I still get the willies thinking about that old Sci-Fi movie about the overgrown ants. I saw it in the 1950s. *Them*, it was called. Shiver, shiver!

I took a break from editing about 5:00 yesterday, walked to the mailbox, and pulled out a familiar red envelope. I cranked up the old computer on which I watch my Netflix movies. I made it until about 5:25, when Scully was poking at a gelatinous corpse. Hit the stop button, ejected the DVD, called Darlene, and said, "How on earth did you talk me into watching an *XFiles* movie?"

"How far did you get?"

I told her.

"I'm surprised you made it that far. It's a good thing it's still light outside!"

Even as we spoke, I slid the stupid DVD back in its little red envelope, and decided to cancel the second XFiles movie, which I was dumb enough to have put on my Netflix queue.

I own very few DVDs, but I just happen to have a copy of *Pride and*

Prejudice. The book has always been a favorite of mine, and even though the movie simplified the story a great deal, I found out last night that *P & P* is a great antidote to *X*.

Now I'm going to have to pull out my print copy of *P&P* and read it again, for the umpteenth time.

Beats *X* any day.

Bees are lucky. They don't ever have to worry about such stuff.

BeeAttitude for Day #387: *Blessed are those who use their imagination rather than letting their imagination use them, for they shall sleep peacefully.*

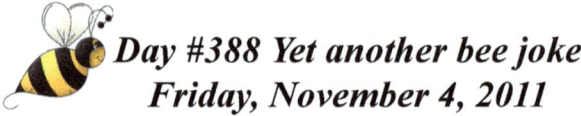
Day #388 Yet another bee joke
Friday, November 4, 2011

After the scary movie post yesterday, it's time for another Bee Joke.

What do you get when you cross a bee with a giraffe?

I'll post your answers in a couple of days.

BeeAttitude for Day #388: *Blessed are those who like to laugh at themselves, for they shall stay sunny.*

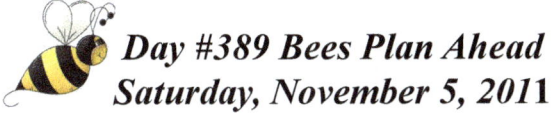 Day #389 Bees Plan Ahead
Saturday, November 5, 2011

Bees and squirrels plan ahead for winter, as evidenced by the heavy combs of honey and pollen, and the full caches of nuts and seeds (many of them taken from my bird feeder!)

But birds don't have that luxury. Their existence, their very survival, is very much a day-to-day affair. Since we humans have wiped out so much of their natural habitat, their existence can be a chancy thing. That's why I feed the birds. In return, they eat a lot of bugs as well as a lot of the seed, suet, and mealworms I provide. Summer is much more fun for me now, what with fewer mosquitoes – thank you, birds!

I've been feeding birds for many years, and I depend on Wild Birds Unlimited in Suwanee GA for my seed and supplies. A great store, with knowledgeable owners and employees, as well as a resident dog (Cheyenne—who was featured in my standalone mystery, *A Slaying Song Tonight*) and a resident cat (Sophie—who was feral, but who adapted to people quite well). *[2019 Note: Sophie's no longer with WBU, but Big Blue has taken her place. Cheyenne has also passed over the Rainbow Bridge, but her influence remains as her "Paw It Forward" program collects thousands of pounds of cat and dog food for local no-kill shelters.]*

© 2011 Kate George

Fran Stewart

If you've read this blog for any length of time, you know I have a lousy camera, so I had to borrow a picture from a writer colleague of mine, Kate George, who posted this photo of a chickadee (and many other bird pictures as well) on her website on Halloween Day.

BeeAttitude for Day #389: *Blessed are those who help our feathered friends, for they shall be even more blessed with music.*

Day #390 And the Question Was...
Sunday, November 6, 2011

Two days ago I asked you *What do you get when you cross a bee with a giraffe*, forgetting that I had already asked that same question some months ago. Honestly, I'd meant to cross this particular bee with a rhinoceros or some other such critter, but it was late at night, and I was beyond sleepy, in that state where the lines of reality blur and morph into something altogether unreal.

You answered it anyway.

One reply came from **Mary** in Iowa, who informed me that she was born and raised on a Texas ranch. "Didn't you ask that same question last February?" she wrote. *[2019 Note: Apparently I don't pay much attention to myself.]* And here's her entry in the bee joke contest:

Combine a bee with a giraffe, and *that thar bee's a tall drink of honey!*

Thanks, Mary. I appreciate your playing the bee joke game and forgiving my brain lapse.

Billy (also from Texas) said the combination would result in *necktar*

And I would imagine there would be lots of that special brand of nectar!

Diana from Colorado went on a scientific bent and wrote that mixing a bee and a giraffe would result in a creature classified as *Apis reticulatum*.

Thank you, Diana. I'm sure your critter will make it into the scientific annals eventually. Maybe. ... Someday ...

BeeAttitude for Day #390: *Blessed are those who accept others for what they are, for they shall relax into the rhythm of the universe.*

Day #391 Boxing and Books and Bees
Monday, November 7, 2011

I know I put bees in the title of this post, but actually, other than the BeeAttitude at the end, there aren't any bees here today.

My friend and fellow writer Jaclyn Weldon White invited me to the book launch of her most recent biography, *The Greatest Champion That Never Was*—the story of W.L. Stripling, who was known in the boxing world of the 1920s and 30s as "Young" Stripling.

When W.L. died, 10,000 people attended his funeral. The city of Macon, Georgia closed all the city playgrounds from 4:00 to 5:00 that day in honor of, as White writes, "the man who had been such a glowing example of sportsmanship and athletic excellence."

It's refreshing to read about people who are the quintessential good guys. In an age that glorifies so many people for the wrong reasons, reading about Young Stripling brings a tear to my eye and a surge of hope to my heart.

BeeAttitude for Day #391: *Blessed are those who read, for whole new worlds shall open to them.*

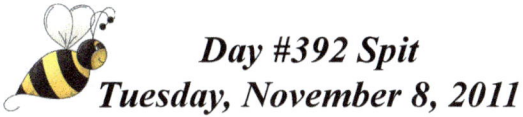
Day #392 Spit
Tuesday, November 8, 2011

I walked down to my backyard creek the other day and pulled out a ripped plastic bag and a broken plastic action figure. I can remember a time when I could drink from streams when my family went on camping trips. Not anymore. Those same streams now are liable to contain oils, bottles, cans, soggy paper, and cigarette butts, as well as pesticide and fertilizer residue from lawns.

People and bees need water for survival. Bees drink a lot of water. If their water sources are polluted, the bees suffer accordingly.

H_2O. Twice as much hydrogen as oxygen, plus vital trace minerals. Wouldn't it be nice if water stayed like that?

In a totally unrelated vein—related only in the fact that spit contains water—I found myself wondering what would happen if ebooks took over the world of publishing. Not that I think that will happen; it was just an idle thought. When people turn page after page of a print book, they almost invariably get to the point where they have to moisten their finger to provide some page-turning traction.

With eBooks, the moisture is not necessary.

What this has to do with anything, I have no idea. Just figured I'd throw the thought out there and see where it fell.

BeeAttitude for Day #392: *Blessed are those who control where their spit lands, for they shall have a cleaner world.*

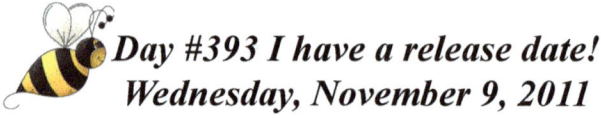
Day #393 I have a release date!
Wednesday, November 9, 2011

My sixth *Biscuit McKee Mystery*, Violet as an Amethyst, is available for preorders. The official release date is December first, but that's not too very far away.

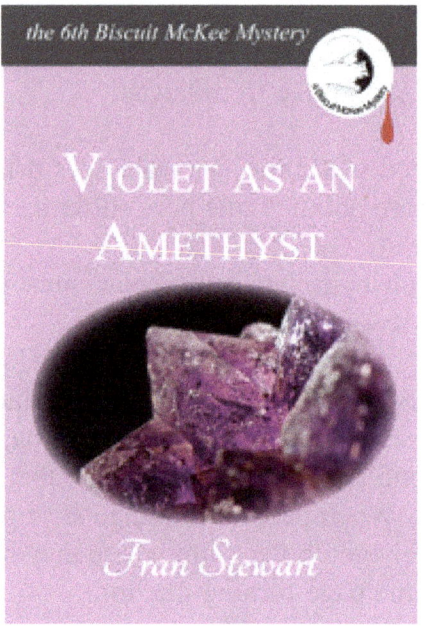

Naturally, Biscuit's husband Bob gets interested in keeping bees, and Biscuit envisions the hives nestled in the corners of their very private back yard. But then, there's this inconveniently dead body…

Here's what it says on the back of the book:
· There isn't a clue as to who pushed librarian Biscuit McKee off the town dock into the raging Metoochie River or whether he will strike again.
· There isn't a clue to the whereabouts of artist Charles Zapota, and his mother is getting frantic.
· There isn't a clue about why Melissa Tarkington's fiancé went to Atlanta for a mysterious meeting or why a lost dog suddenly latches onto Biscuit's sister, Glaze.
· VIOLET AS AN AMETHYST continues the saga of small-town Mar-

tinsville, as Biscuit's life is threatened by the deadly intent of one particular man.

Sneak Preview—the start of *Violet as an Amethyst* ©2011 by Fran Stewart

It *was* a dark and stormy night, dammit, and I was stuck, gasping for air, desperate for warmth, wedged between two branches of a drowning pine tree as the rain-swollen Metoochie River tried its best to uproot the almost completely submerged tree and drown me. If it didn't freeze me first.

I had no idea who had pushed me from the dock, but I knew I hadn't simply slipped. A moment after I'd sensed I wasn't the only one standing there watching the surge of the storm water, two big hands hit the middle of my back.

What on earth had I been thinking to take a walk at 2 a.m. when I could have stayed curled up next to Bob? Obviously I'd lost my mind, and now I was paying for it.

I prayed for a convenient lightning bolt to strike the man who'd pushed me, whoever he was. I prayed for dawn. I prayed for a friendly boater or a sudden river-drying drought. My only chance was to hang on and hope for rescue. I screamed for help again and again, but heard no answer above the roar of the river. Visions of Snoopy, pounding away at his typewriter on top of his redroofed cartoon doghouse, careened around inside my muddled head. It was a dark and stormy night; it was a dark and stormy night. I couldn't get beyond that first stupid sentence.

I'd been sound asleep, in the middle of a very satisfying dream, when Marmalade had padded up my leg, over the curve of my hip, and wiggled her way under my arm. Breathing is difficult with a cat against one's nose, so I'd shifted onto my back. She shifted with me and placed her paw over my eyelid. It's hard not to wake up when that happens.

Look outside the window.

I swear, in the middle of the night her purr sounds like a dump truck.

Someone is in the backyard beyond the fence.

I pushed her out of the way—gently, but firmly. "Let me sleep, Marmy," I mumbled. Bob stirred, muttered something but didn't seem to wake up, and settled back down. "Go 'way," I said again as she balanced on my hip like Snoopy on his doghouse roof, and continued to nudge me with her paws and her head.

Come to the window. Come to the window now.

"Shh! Don't wake up Bob."

Now!

When she let out one of her gurgly yarps I gave in. "Awright, Marms." I considered pulling the blanket over my head, but knew she'd never let me get away with it. "What's going on? Did you find a mouse?" I slipped into my robe and stretched as she jumped down and bounded to the big window.

And so on . . . I hope you'll consider reading my Biscuit McKee mysteries—and tell your friends about them!

BeeAttitude for Day #393: *Blessed are those who read, for they shall learn much about their world through the eyes of others.*

Day #394 CPA, Attack Dogs, Bees and Spiders
Thursday, November 10, 2011

Right after a baby bee emerges from the cell where she grew from an egg to a larva to a pupa to a worker bee, she starts about doing her work, all the various jobs she's going to handle over her life span of six weeks. I've talked about this process before, and I'm in awe of how orderly the entire process is.

But what about the learning curve? I've read that baby spiders have to practice web making. Their first efforts tend to be lopsided, poorly anchored, too small, and with the strands too far apart (or too close together). Yes, they have the instinct to build those webs. But instinct needs a little help.

I've never read anything about how bees learn. Are their first efforts less than precise? I've never seen a honeycomb where the cells were square instead of hexagonal. I've never seen cells that were too small to hold the pupae. Are the bees absolutely correct from the moment they're born? If I as a beekeeper try to invade a hive, will a newly born baby bee try to sting me? Or will she leave that job to the grownup bees? Does she know she'll die if she stings me?

And what about people's learning curves? We have BIG issues around that. Are people born with the instinct to protect their own? Or do they have to develop that skill?

Last year, as you may know, I took the Citizen's Police Academy, and learned a great deal about the ways in which the officers learn to protect the citizenry. Are people who go into police work simply those who have a more highly developed protection instinct than the rest of us? I don't know. But here's your chance to explore the possibilities.

Remember last January when I posted those pictures of me in the Michelin Man suit—ain't it purty?—being attacked by a police dog as part of the Gwinnett Citizens Police Academy? You, too, can make a fashion statement like this ...

The Gwinnett County (Georgia) Police Department sponsors two Citizen Police Academies each year. To apply, go to www.gwinnettcpa.com

If you don't live in Gwinnett County Georgia, then please check your local police department to see if they offer a citizens academy. It will be well worth your time.

Spread the word! The "Michelin Woman & the Dog" routine is entirely optional.

BeeAttitude for Day #394: *Blessed are those who try new flowers, for they shall find nectar aplenty.*

Day #395 What Are We Doing to Our World?
Friday, November 11, 2011

On 11/11/11, it seems fitting to talk about the insanity of people who believe that killing is the answer. It's not only people we kill with our wars.

The phrase, *man's inhumanity to man* has, unfortunately, become a common one. Our inhumanity stretches farther than simply to other people.

November 11th (Veterans Day) was set aside as a time to remember the war that was supposed to have ended all wars. I'll let the irony of that statement speak for itself.

There are, unfortunately, many "wars" being fought on many different fronts—some as small as our own back yards.

Doggone it. I can try as much as possible to make my yard and my neighborhood safe for bees and birds and other small critters, but then a chemical giant comes along, pays for research that says, "Oh yes, this product is perfectly safe for honeybees," publishes that research, and expects everyone to believe it.

The unfortunate truth is that people DO believe such lies.

Bayer – the company that makes the aspirin on your shelf – also produces neonicitinoid pesticides. I hope they concoct the two products in separate buildings. Their *clothianidin* pesticide (the nasty pink stuff in the jars shown in this 2008 picture) was touted to be perfectly safe for honeybees. I even saw an advertising film where company officials bragged about its safety, based on "the very best research." Research, it turns out, the folks at Bayer had hired out to their own researchers.

Caption: In early May 2008, between 330 and 500 million bees were killed in the Western part of Germany (Rheintal) by Bayer's clothianidin pesticide, which had been applied as a dressing to amize seed. More than 7,000 beekeeper rang up the Landesverband Badischer Imker (beekeepers' union) to report total losses. *[2019 note: I originally found this picture and the related information at a website called bayerkillsbees. Unfortunately, it no longer seems to be available.]*

In the spring of 2008, millions of bees in Germany died as a result of clothianidin. I know that sounds like old news, but this kind of devastation continues to happen, and not only in Europe. One of the members of our bee club lives close enough to a particular small farm where the unenlightened owner sprays all sorts of toxins with reckless abandon. She said she's extremely tired of coming home from work and finding entire hives wiped out.

When will we humans wake up to what we're doing to our world?

Closer to home, Dan Rather presented a report in September of 2011 which revealed that all those reports from the multinational Bayer corporation that told us their systemic pesticides were safe for bees contained a wee problem. A wee problem with far-ranging consequences.

The test fields covered only 2 acres. The bees from a hive forage over about a thousand acres. Therefore, the bees that were killed by the pesticides in those 2 acres pretty much disappeared from the results because so many of the foragers were gathering from the other 998 acres around their hive. To find the full report, you can go to panna.org/blog/danratherpesticidesbees

Just as I encourage people to check out forwarded emails with www.snopes.com to prevent infecting friends' e-boxes with garbage, so I'd like to find a way we could know whether "research" is valid.

Even better would be if the folks doing the "research" would act with integrity.

Is that too much to ask?

BeeAttitude for Day #395: *Blessed are those who treat our Mother Earth with respect. We bees appreciate them.*

Day #396 And the Winners Were (Not) ...
Saturday, November 12, 2011

When the winner of the dog drawing was chosen, I emailed all the other people who had entered and asked them to send me pictures I could post on my blog. That way their dogs would at least be "published," even if they hadn't made it into the next Biscuit McKee mystery. Only four people took me up on that offer, so here are four of the dogs who didn't win.

The first photo below is Bella, but she reminds Cathy of her dog Bingo from childhood. Cathy said if she'd won, she would have asked me to put Bingo in the book.

Next comes Sally's 11-year-old dog, whose name is Ginger:

This is Annie, who adopted Dauna:

And finally Radar (a glorious Italian Spinone, a breed with which I wasn't familiar) lives with Marni. If great big Radar had won I would have had a lot of rewriting to do in the final scenes, but I would have thoroughly enjoyed doing it:

Lots of other people entered their dogs in the drawing, but you'll just have to imagine what they look like.

The winner of the drawing was Gracie.

Her bio and photo will appear in VIOLET AS AN AMETHYST

BeeAttitude for Day #396: *Blessed are those who love bees and dogs, for they shall always have the fuzzies in their lives.*

[2019 note: Marmalade and Wooly Bear and Fuzzy Britches all suggest that cats should bee in this list as well.]

Fran Stewart

Day #397 New Windows & Well Hived Bees
Sunday, November 13, 2011

Friday I had the fine folks from Weather Tite Windows take out all my old windows and put in new ones. [**2019 Note:** *see day #354.*]

I'm not sitting here shivering.

I was shivering plenty on Friday, though. You see, in order to put in new windows efficiently, one first has to take out all the old ones, prepare the openings, set in the new windows, and then do the caulking.

Brrr!

I was wearing my long johns, a turtleneck, and another sweater underneath my sweat pants and sweat shirt. I had two knit caps, and a scarf around my neck. The good news is that because it was so cold, the bees were all keeping warm in their wild adopted hives, so we didn't have to worry about any of them flying through the window-sized holes in my walls.

I heated up a big bowl of chili for my lunch just so I could hold the hot bowl in my hands. Even through the mittens, the warmth was appreciated.

Was it worth it, though? You bet! My bay window looked like this before they started:

Halfway through the process it was like this:

And this is what I ended up with:

Ain't it gorgeous? None of those black squares marring the sight. What a shame to have to put my curtains back up.

And just a word about my newest book: The preorders are coming in regularly, according to word from my publisher. The very first preorder came from someone in Scotland! (The woman whose dog, Radar, didn't win the contest. *See yesterday's post.*)

BeeAttitude for Day #397: *Blessed are those who do what they need to in order to stay warm through the winter, for they, like we bees, shall be toasty.*

Day #398 Houses Gone, but Hives Here
Monday, November 14, 2011

A week or so ago I bought *Gone: a Heartbreaking Story of the Civil War / A Photographic Plea for Preservation,* featuring the photographs of Nell Dickerson who has, with her camera, chronicled the sorry state of many old buildings. On the jacket leaf, Dickerson says, "What the war didn't take, time and apathy did. And yet those grand old homes—whether mansion or cabin—deserve our reverence and protection."

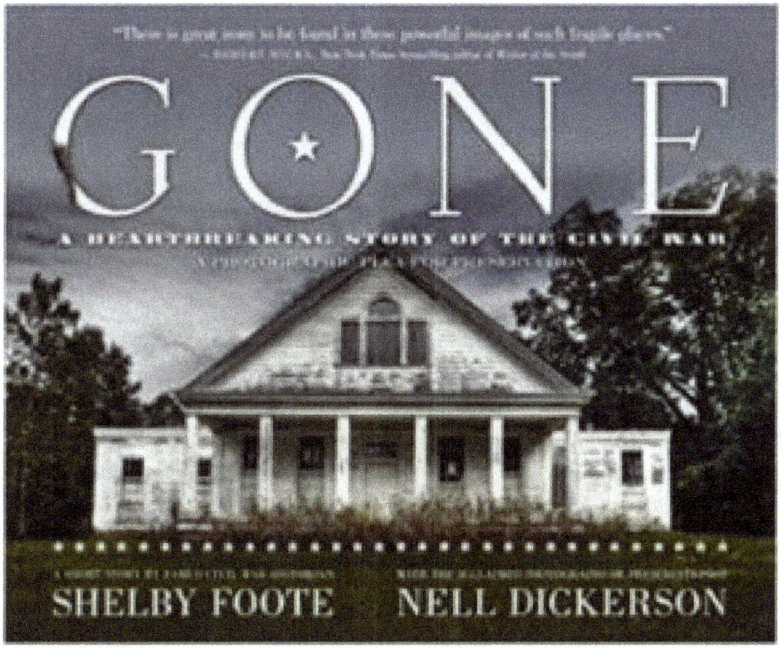

As I paged through the book yesterday, I began to wonder about beehives. Are they ever simply abandoned? Well, yes. That's the hallmark of colony collapse disorder – the abandoning of a hive. Like the Anasazi of the Southwest, the bees simply leave and nobody knows why.

But if we're not dealing with a disorder, then bees keep their hives going, year after year after year. When they get too crowded, half the colony leaves with their queen. The remaining half hatch a new queen, and life in the hive goes on.

When I had to give away my two hives, the forager bees who were left behind took their nectar and pollen with them and were welcomed into wild hives.

I keep saying we could learn something from bees. They don't use wars to settle disputes; they model the precepts of personal responsibility; they contribute to the health of the world.

I'll say it again – we could learn something from bees.

BeeAttitude for Day #398: *Blessed are those who treasure their hives, for they shall find honey in multiple places.*

BeesKnees #4: A Beekeeping Memoir

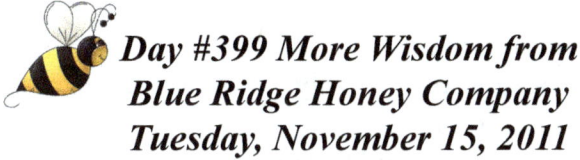 *Day #399 More Wisdom from Blue Ridge Honey Company*
Tuesday, November 15, 2011

I'd like to take today to quote extensively from the Blue Ridge Honey Company website. I took this whole little essay from the Blue Ridge site, and I've taken the liberty of bolding several sentences. You're welcome to read the whole thing – or just the parts I've emphasized.

While you're reading, though, why don't you munch on some toast and honey!
=========

A PERSONAL NOTE
We would like to encourage honey buyers to purchase U.S. honey whether it be from us or someone else.

The Beekeeping Industry in this country is very important and, without it, much of the agriculture in this country could not exist.

About one third of the food in an average grocery store, as well as a large portion of the produce department, depends on honeybee pollination.

Over the years we have been involved in the pollination of alfalfa, almonds, cranberries, cucumbers, apples, crimson clover, Dutch white clover, sweet clover, squash, pumpkins, pears, cherries, strawberries, sunflowers, radish seed, cabbage seed, watermelons, cantaloupe, plums and more.

There are many other crops that depend on honeybee pollination and, without them, the store shelf would look much different.

Although beekeepers get paid for much of the pollination that occurs, they could not survive without the income from honey sales.

U.S. beekeepers are often offered prices that are below the cost of production and many go out of business each year. The answer for this is for domestic honey to be in demand. Much of the honey consumed in this country is imported. And that is okay.

We do not produce enough honey to meet the demand in this country and some of the imported honey is a good, high quality product. Examples of this are imports from Canada, Australia, New Zea-

land, Germany, and others.

However, there is also a lot of highly questionable, extremely cheap honey coming into this country.

Many countries do not have the laws and regulations in place, nor do they care enough, to keep their honey uncontaminated and pure.

In recent years, huge amounts of honey have shown up here, especially from some countries in Asia and South America, that have been highly adulterated with other sweeteners such as high fructose corn syrup and also contain chemicals and antibiotics that are illegal to use in this country. It is hard to compete with this.

Our best hope is to raise awareness and promote our own product.

Our own National Honey Board is only able to promote honey generically and is not allowed to promote U.S. Honey as such. So, we have to toot our own horn.

We are not trying to suggest that domestic honey is perfect or goes without incident, but the chance of getting a quality product with U.S. honey is much better than most imports, especially when purchased from a reputable producer.

If you purchase honey from us, we really appreciate your business, and we sincerely hope you enjoy our product. If you purchase from someone else, we hope you enjoy theirs, too.

Quality honey, in its purest form, is one of the finest foods on planet earth. It is very good for us.

That having been said, I would like to encourage everyone to eat and enjoy more honey.

Bob Binnie
Blue Ridge Honey Company
Lakemont, GA
==========

BeeAttitude for Day #399: *Blessed are those who know what they eat, for they shall thrive.*

Day #400 Immune Systems and Weeds in the Front Yard
Wednesday, November 16, 2011

People have internal immune systems.

If we ingest something that's bad for us, or if a germ gets inside us, we have all sorts of little processes that go to work to protect us.

If we're relatively healthy and relatively free of the toxins that seem to pervade our culture, we have a pretty good chance of staving off whatever it is that aims to take us down.

Bees do not have internal immune systems. All their protection is external.

Think about that next time you're tempted to spray some toxic chemical on your lawn to get rid of unsightly weeds.

Why don't we change our definition of *unsightly*? After all, our lawns would probably be healthier and last longer if they were made up of those thriving local plants that lawn maintenance companies (and homeowner associations) like to call weeds. I'd love to see lawns rife with clover, for instance.

I admit this would take some major reeducation.

But think of all the bees it would save…

BeeAttitude for Day #400: *Blessed are those who avoid poisons, for they shall pass a healthier world on to their children.*

www.ingramcontent.com/pod-product-compliance
Lightning Source LLC
Chambersburg PA
CBHW071709020426
42333CB00017B/2199